D1756432

Linkedin

For

College

Students

U.C.B.
LIBRARY

Debra Faris

BARNSLEY COLLEGE

00135431

30001992

Linkedin for College Students
Published by
SEGR Publishing LLC
2150 Northwest Hwy., #114-1168
Grapevine, TX 76051
www.SEGRPublishing.com

© 2014 Debra Faris
All rights reserved

First edition printed March 2014

All rights reserved. Except as permitted by applicable copyright laws, no part of this book may be reproduced, duplicated, sold or distributed in any form or by any means, either mechanical, by photocopy, electronic, or by computer, or stored in a database or retrieval system, without the express written permission of the publisher/authors, except for brief quotations by reviewers.

ISBN: 978-1-61920-026-5
Printed in the United States of America

Library of Congress Control Number: 2014946967

This is a work of non-fiction. The ideas presented are those of the author alone. All references to possible results to be gained from the techniques discussed in this book relate to specific past examples and are not necessarily representative of any future results specific individuals may achieve. Information presented is correct to the best knowledge of the author at the time of publication.

The author of this book has no connection of any kind whatsoever with LinkedIn Corporation or any of its subsidiaries or allied companies. LinkedIn Corporation has given no endorsement of the strategies outlined in this book, implied or explicit.

Contents

Introduction

In today's world, where things are so easily, instantly obtainable on the Internet, it's necessary to bring back old-world traditional relationship-building. *Linkedin for College Students* was crafted to teach students the necessary skills to build long-term relationships with the right people through networking, engagement, and follow-up.

In addition, this book will teach them the entrepreneurial and leadership skills necessary to develop "an eye for opportunity." They will develop their underlying intuitive skills, which are the basis of all human connections, enabling them to build productive, long-term relationships that will shape their destiny.

The *Character Assessment* section in the first chapter will help students understand and share who they are as individuals as well as their unique gifts. They will learn how these gifts can be nurtured and encouraged in specific employment positions. The processes in the book will assist them to successfully match their college educations with job opportunities and, even more importantly, their personalities with company cultures.

Acknowledgements

Thank you to all the people who were instrumental
in helping create this book:

Thank you, Lee Pound for being my mentor, chief editor, design
and layout person, and book coach, giving me the vision and
understanding of things I never understood before.

Thank you, Bob Donnell for being the person who cared for me
knowing that I lost my son. You are the coach of coaches.

Thank you, Bob Bare, my publisher, who believed
in my book enough to publish it.

Thank you, Jack C Crawford. As circumstances happened, my
computer crashed and Jack got me a new computer
so I could finish my book.

Thank you all the people who have influenced
and contributed to my life.

Dedication

In Memory of my son

Phillip Miguel Godwin

10/29/89 – 07/11/11

My son Phil loved snowboarding, Lake Tahoe, California, his baby girls, and his fiancée, Denise. I am inspired to write this book in memory of my son. He aspired to become an anthropologist. His life was cut short and it broke my heart. His one little baby girl was only eight months old and the other baby girl was born four months after he passed the day before his birthday. I wished for a way to make a difference to help others.

Months after my son's death, I woke up in the middle of my sleep at 3 a.m. I had been contemplating writing a LinkedIn book for all the C-level people I had been coaching who were in transition looking for a job.

In that middle of the night moment, I realized that they had in some cases spent tens of thousands of dollars in college tuition fees on their kids' education. When these kids graduated, they would need not just a job but also the relationship skills needed to get the job. I knew in that instant that LinkedIn was the answer and *Linkedin for College Students* was born. Now that book has life as you read it.

I hope and pray that in this book I can "make a difference" in some way – somehow. I wish you much success in your education, continuing growth, career, and path in life. I hope that this book and its many time-tested strategies will lead many to rich and fulfilled lives. I will remember Phil and know that because of my personal loss, in some measure I found the inspiration to encourage you to greatness.

Remember the greatness and genius you see in others is also in you:)

Debra Faris, CNO aka Ms LinkedIn
The Chief Networking Officer

1

What's my purpose on LinkedIn?

We will receive not what we idly wish for but what we justly earn.
Our rewards will always be in exact proportion to our service.
--Earl Nightingale

Why LinkedIn?

Facebook, Twitter, Google+, Instagram, LinkedIn, Pinterest, Tumblr, Flickr, MySpace, Meetup; the list goes on and on. Social media sites are cropping up left and right on the internet and are here to stay. People interact and connect on social media sites, forming virtual communities and networks, and share information and ideas. With all these choices, why use LinkedIn?

You may think LinkedIn is only for people in business and wonder what difference it can make for you. You're a college student; business is the farthest thing from your mind. The answer is simple. LinkedIn is about building relationships and deep connections. In college you build relationships both online and offline with your fellow students, your teachers and professors, and other faculty members. You deepen these relationships by connecting with them on LinkedIn. Then you expand your connections and relationships using LinkedIn. You build a team of connections and relationships that will help you in the future as you search for a job in the professional world.

Although relationships and connections are important in college, they are far more critical in business. The best way to find a job after you graduate is through connections, both who you know and who knows you.

> *Singleness of purpose is one of the chief essentials for success in life, no matter what may be one's aim.*
>
> **John D. Rockefeller, Jr.**

When you build a team of individuals who know you, like you, and want to help you, you make finding the right job far easier. LinkedIn is the perfect place to start. When you build your business profile while you are still in college, you are building your future business persona. People begin to learn what you're all about.

Start now. In today's competitive job market, you cannot afford to be left behind. College students need to use and become experts at LinkedIn long before graduation. Building profiles that represent who you are, show your authenticity and character, and showcase your talents and awards gives the business world a glimpse of what to expect as you enter the job force. When you go into the real world, you will enter the job market with connections that can help you get the career or the business you want. The quickest way to make this happen is to use your college years to build those relationships.

If you are already in business or just graduating from college, you need to share your special expertise so the world knows who you are and what you can do. LinkedIn is your tool for spreading that message. Its members' names appear at the top of Google search rankings because it has 300,000,000 members, massive traffic, and constant change in content. It even outranks websites people have paid tens of thousands of dollars to create. This gives you a big advantage when potential employers or customers search for you. In addition, LinkedIn's wide range of privacy options allows you to control what others see about you.

I call LinkedIn your mini-website because it gives you many of the same benefits as having your own website. You can connect and build relationships, get your needs shared, and showcase your skills and talents.

LinkedIn offers many avenues to create and discover your ideal job or future clients. That's why I suggest you build your profile in three parts.

1.) First, complete the basics and develop a "complete" profile on LinkedIn.
2.) Second, design your profile so busy executives can read it easily.
3.) Third, show your personality and your connection with the real world in a way that gives you high credibility and attracts the right people to you.

Even though LinkedIn is designed as a way for business owners, executives, and professionals to connect, do business, and find jobs, it is still social media. Many people think it is enough to put up their profiles, which are all about themselves, and expect to attract the people they want without interacting. This is the wrong approach. To get from point A to point B with potential connections, you must communicate with them. Business is all about talking with people, creating connections, and building communities. To succeed on LinkedIn, you must create engagement and community.

When a client of mine says, "I thought this wasn't social media," I say, "That's what I thought in the beginning, too. Then I found out I was wrong and became very excited with the opportunities the site offered."

When you see these opportunities, you will think, "Oh My Gosh, Gold, Gold, Gold, Gold!" LinkedIn is the most phenomenal site I have ever seen. That's because you get tons of free publicity with your LinkedIn profile. When you get started as a college student, you will build an edge over your competition for the best positions after you graduate. Fill in each section to its highest potential and become a LinkedIn professional before you even leave college.

300 Million Members in 200 Countries

WIKIPEDIA
The Free Encyclopedia

Article Talk   Read Edit View

LinkedIn

From Wikipedia, the free encyclopedia
(Redirected from Linkedin)

Main page
Contents
Featured content
Current events
Random article
Donate to Wikipedia
Wikimedia Shop

▾ Interaction
  Help
  About Wikipedia
  Community portal
  Recent changes
  Contact page

LinkedIn / lɪŋkt. ɪn/ is a business-oriented social networking service. Founded in December 2002 and launched on May 5, 2003,[3] it is mainly used for professional networking. In 2006, LinkedIn increased to 20 million viewers.[7] As of June 2013, LinkedIn reports more than 259 million acquired users in more than 200 countries and territories.[2][8]

The site is available in 20 languages,[2] including English, French, German, Italian, Portuguese, Spanish, Dutch, Swedish, Danish, Romanian, Russian, Turkish, Japanese, Czech, Polish, Korean, Indonesian, Malay, and Tagalog.[9][10] As of 2 July 2013, Quantcast reports LinkedIn has 65.6 million monthly unique U.S. visitors and 178.4 million globally,[11] a number that as of 29 October 2013 has increased to 184 million.[12] In June 2011, LinkedIn had 33.9 million unique visitors, up 63 percent from

If you haven't decided to jump into LinkedIn, this book will show you how to get started and the benefits you will receive. LinkedIn is a unique channel that gives the consumer multiple dimensions and tons of value, all for free. It has no hosting fee and no monthly membership fee (although members can pay for an upgrade account which gives a few perks and extra benefits).

Be sure to ask yourself these questions. What is your intention on LinkedIn? Is it to find a job or connect with old college friends? Is it to find groups that can help you market your products or services? Is your network going to be online or offline or both? Identify the people you want to meet and the message you want to send. Then connect, follow up and be part of the communities that keep you connected.

Mike Ferry   1st

Real Estate Coaching | Real Estate Training | 19K+
Connections | Top 1% on LinkedIn | CEO-Mike Ferry
Organization

Las Vegas, Nevada Area   Real Estate

Current   The Mike Ferry Organization
Previous   Nightingale-Conant
Education   School of Hard Knocks

Send a message ▼   500+

My Influencers: Mike Ferry™

I will share with you throughout this book that through many years of meeting incredible people, experiencing amazing coincidences, and being in the right place at the right time, I have had the opportunity to develop lasting relationships which have helped me in many ways on LinkedIn. Whether you want to call this first story a coincidence or being at the right place at the right time, it is one of my favorites because it is about one of the top coaches in the world, who is a prime example of purpose, authenticity and transparency.

My story with Mike Ferry™ started more than 30 years ago when at the age of 21, I attended one of his real estate Superstar retreats. Mike was known as the non-nonsense coach who made struggling Realtors into profitable business people. He's called a tough coach, because he says it like it is. Have you ever heard that the truth can set you free? When many people go to seminars and events, they think they are there to get better, but in reality it is because they want to feel better.

When I walked into the room and saw the crowd of over 3,000 people, I thought, "This guy must be really-really good."

He started with, "I've heard all the stories and the excuses and frankly ladies and gentlemen, they won't make you successful. If you're ready to be successful I expect you to take notes or go home, otherwise you're wasting your time and mine."

Let's just say, "NO ONE!!! left the room."

I listened intently, eagerly writing down every word he said, impatient to get back home and implement his action plan. I remember Mike saying, "Don't fix something that's not broken."

I've seen people try to do it their own way versus listening to the coach who has a proven winning formula. It's a formula for disaster. I chose to stick to Mike's plan, which was to write your goals down and know your numbers. One of my goals was that by my birthday month I would list 21 properties in one month, which I did. I went on to become a top producer for the next 24 consecutive months in a company of 500 Realtors.

> *When I chased after money, I never had enough. When I got my life on purpose and focused on giving of myself and everything that arrived into my life, then I was prosperous.*
> **Wayne Dyer**

As the years passed, Mike Ferry™ and his organization have mentored over one million Realtors. Although the average Realtor makes $6,000 per year, I have seen Mike's agents go from $50K to $100K, $100K to $200K, $250K to $500K up to agents who have made a million dollars in a single year.

Whichever field or industry you endeavor to enter, read books and study those who are successful when you are young. It is much easier to create a pattern of good habits that lead you closer to your goals, than to break old bad habits that didn't move you in your desired direction.

As life comes full circle, I got the opportunity to connect with Mike again thanks to LinkedIn. In a lot of ways, I was still living by the high value skills I had learned from Mike so many years ago. I was now the Michael Jordan of LinkedIn, reading through thousands and thousands of profiles. I was coaching people in transition (people looking for a job) including C-level executives like Chief Executive Officers (CEOs), Chief Financial Officers (CFOs), Chief Operations Officers (COOs). I maintained a consistent high level of service and studied my craft deeply so I could better help others meet their goals.

When Mike reached out to me on LinkedIn, I was excited because I had kept the high standards I learned from him so many years ago in my new work. One of my favorite lessons is, "How you do one thing is how you do everything." When you are starting out, learn how to do things right the first time.

It was a great privilege and the honor to work with the Mike Ferry™ Organization for six months. Mike taught me how to fish for myself, be honest with myself, and be true to my purpose. He has built the largest real estate tribe on LinkedIn. He is always on purpose and authentic as he helps Realtors become the best in their industry. Mike's LinkedIn has evolved to over 20,000 first level connections, 1,500 members in his "Mike Ferry™ Realtor Connection" group on LinkedIn, and over 1,500 past clients and fans honor him on LinkedIn.

> *You can have anything you want — if you want it badly enough. You can be anything you want to be, have anything you desire, accomplish anything you set out to accomplish — if you will hold to that desire with singleness of purpose.*
> **Robert Collier**

In this book, I will use a lot of different industries as examples. You may think these are not your industries. Not so! These principles are universal. The biggest benefit to you is that others in your industry will not know these success tips, which can be the differentiation you need to stand out from your competition.

I attribute my success to two key lessons Mike teaches in his seminars, that mindset is the most important attribute you have and that consistency and discipline will get you the results you desire. He teaches you to ask the right questions and that these questions will lead you to the right answers to get the right results. What does this have to do with LinkedIn? You build and post a profile because you want the right people to find you. This is local search engine optimization. When you create the various sections of your profile, add words that your tribe will use when they search for you on LinkedIn. Once you've built your profile, you invite people you know or respect to become connections, which then turn into relationships similar to my relationship with Mike Ferry™. Those connections and relationships will assist you as you move from the collegiate world into the working world.

Online, Offline

The most successful online, offline internet communication vehicles are in the infamous dating world led by companies like EHarmony and Match.com, which allow their members to seek relationships that fit their criteria, ranging from friendships to dating to meeting someone with whom they can spend their rest of their life. LinkedIn works in a similar fashion except it is centered in the business world. You connect with other members, build relationships, and use those relationships in your career.

> *Everyone has a purpose in life … a unique gift of special talent to give others. And when we blend this unique talent with service to others, we experience the ecstasy and exultation of our own spirit, which is the ultimate goal of all goals.*
>
> **Deepak Chopra**

Each time you look at LinkedIn and its members, you will find people that interest you and people you want to connect with. Maybe someone shared how they accomplished goals in a specific position, or maybe the groups they joined might interest or benefit you. These are all ways to connect with other human beings. You can also see employment histories, where people started and how their careers advanced through the years from, for example, a copy clerk to Senior VP of the Western Region for a billion-dollar company. As you continue to search and explore, you see life and careers from a different perspective.

You can incorporate your offline connections in LinkedIn as well. Connect with your family, friends, and professors as you begin to build your network. Since you already have a relationship with these offline connections who are like you, start with them. Then as you work on college committees, become valued interns, or study for a semester abroad, add the connections you make during these events to your profile. That will build your online connections and build your bucket. Expand your profile as you expand your life. Don't underestimate any connection. Sometimes one odd connection can lead to your dream job. Use LinkedIn to foster both your online connections and your offline connections. Build your networks and develop relationships that help you accomplish what you desire.

Authenticity and Transparency

Building an authentic profile on LinkedIn requires skill and evaluation. To show people who you really are, you need to dig into your character traits, values, and skill sets and make sure that the image you're painting for viewers represents you. The more authentic you make your profile, the more value your connections will have to you. You only get one chance to make a first impression. Be true to yourself and allow your readers to get a feel for who you are.

At a Tony Robbins seminar many years ago, the three most important things I learned were to know your purpose, know your intention, and that questions are the answer. I got off track many times, slowed down, collected myself, and started to ask better questions, which led to better results. Nobody can change your results for you. You are the only one who can change your life and you do it by asking, "What results did I get and how could I do it differently to get better results?"

Einstein said, "If you keep doing the same thing over and over, you will keep getting the same result. That's called insanity!" This is why questions are the key to a powerful LinkedIn profile.

You may ask, "How can a college student have a profile without having job experience?" You are more than just your job experience, so, in a following section, I want you to ask, "Who Am I?" which will begin your journey on your new path.

Mission and Mindset

Ever been on a mission? Maybe it's a mission to see your favorite movie, a mission to eat a whole pizza, a mission to meet that cute girl in your chemistry class and start a new life, or a mission to get a job and begin contributing to the world as your college career comes to an end. It is important to know your mission and purpose for connecting on LinkedIn before you start. If you start with the end in mind, setting up your profile and making important connections will create a more effective message. Know why you're on LinkedIn and what you want to accomplish before you start and your outcome will be aligned with your goal.

Character isn't something you were born with and can't change, like your fingerprints. It's something you weren't born with and must take responsibility for forming.

Jim Rohn

Mindsets are beliefs about yourself and your most basic qualities. Think about your intelligence, your personality and your talents. Are these qualities fixed traits that can never be changed or are these traits that you can change and cultivate throughout your life?

There are two basic types of mindsets, fixed mindset and growth mindset. A person with a fixed mindset believes that their basic traits are fixed qualities that they cannot change. With a growth mindset people believe that their most basic abilities can be developed through dedication and hard work.

So, you ask, how does this relate to LinkedIn? The mindset that you approach LinkedIn with will dictate your results. Just like life, if you approach LinkedIn without understanding all its dimensions and details and don't use its flexibility, you will wind up with results different than you expected. Those who think they can set up a pretty profile and that people and jobs will flock to them automatically are sure to be disappointed.

However you approach LinkedIn, remember it is a mindset connecting with others and building relationships. Mike Ferry™ teaches a course called *Mindset, Skills, Action, and Motivation* that shows people how all of these components work together for success. You start with the right mindset and the rest falls into place. If you approach LinkedIn with the mindset and strategy of knowing where you want to go, who you need to meet, and ask the right questions as you build your profile, you will find LinkedIn to be a valuable tool in your networking and career search.

I once shared a story about my skydiving adventure with a CFO (chief financial officer). He said, "Who would jump out of a perfectly good airplane?" That was his mindset. He wanted to keep his feet on the ground.

I said, "I understand why you might feel that way. But I did it, you didn't. Wouldn't you like to know what I learned from it?"

Even if you never plan to jump out of an airplane, you can still benefit from the knowledge I gained and how I felt. Everyone has their own mindset. Sometimes it benefits you to take on someone else's mindset or at least share their experience so you can learn from it.

When I finished, my friend/client said he didn't realize he was looking through such a narrow perspective and that he would have missed possibilities for collaboration. He is a left-brain expert, analytical and detailed, where I have a creative, exploratory, communicative, curious side; therefore when we collaborate, we bring added value, whether in a company or a relationship.

Who Am I? I am...!

Who am I? Have you ever sat in your dorm room on a quiet Sunday afternoon and pondered that question? You know your name and what city you came from and what you look like. But when you really get right down to it...Who am I? And once I figure out who I am, how do I tell everyone else?

When we graduate from high school and move on to college, trade schools, or careers, many of us are quick to pick a career and jump in. We might do what the family has done and go to Law School, become a fourth generation florist, or maybe become a dentist to join Dad's practice. Many people do this without thinking about their passions and never take time to outline their desires and visions.

When this happens, a progression of jobs creates a career and before we know it we are in our early thirties, burned out, unhappy with what we're doing, and living unfulfilled lives.

To succeed, you must learn the truth of who you are. If you've taken philosophy classes, you know Socrates' famous quote, "Know Thyself." This is one of the deepest truths in life. You must know who you are before you can achieve a happy, fulfilled life.

Man masters nature not by force but by understanding.
Jacob Bronowski

People don't understand the significance of the many bits and pieces that make up their lives. They think one job was a waste of time or didn't benefit them or that a boss was too harsh. Later in life they realize that everything they ever did made them the people they are today.

For instance, being a Boy Scout or a Girl Scout gives you training in honor, trust and integrity. Those attitudes will follow you as you move into responsible positions such as Manager, Director, CEO or CFO. Past opportunities create benefits for an individual's future, because in the end it's all about your character.

You need to portray your character in your LinkedIn profile; because if you do it correctly you will send a powerful message to the people you want to connect with. Identify key character traits that describe you and incorporate them into your profile. The more your profile reflects your genuine self in an authentic and transparent way, the more chances you have of connecting with the audience you desire. You need to find keywords that identify who you are, what you like, and what you want. You will recognize these words when they resonate with you. If you think about the word for more than five seconds, it belongs in your profile. Keywords that resonate with you and describe who you are create an in-depth LinkedIn profile that will attract the people you want to connect with as you embark on your professional career.

The next questions you need ask are: What are the goals of your connections? What are your goals for the communication you will have with people on LinkedIn? What are the goals of the communities you are part of?

Make a very clear statement that says, "Here's who I am and here's who my clients are." If you are in finance, write down all those characteristics, print out profiles of about 100 other financial people, and highlight all the things that resonate for you.

When you ask yourself these questions, you begin to think about the message the people reading your profile are receiving. What does your profile communicate about you and how will your audience interpret that message? If your message isn't clear to you, it won't be clear to them. Put yourself in their position; think like your recruiter. Does your profile show off your talents, strengths, and accomplishments? If not, fix it! This is your opportunity to brag about yourself. If you're not confident doing that (a lot of us aren't), have a friend read your profile and ask for their input. Listen as they brag about you; include their words in your profile. You're amazing and everyone deserves to know about you!

Ensure that you read your profile once you have completed it and that it conveys the correct message in the correct tone. You want to attract people to you and increase your chance to build relationships. If your profile is poorly worded or unattractive, it may cost you the jobs, orders, business, relationships, or closeness that you want. You only get one chance to make a first impression. Make your profile shine and shout out your greatness.

Let's recap

*The **words of character** that resonate with me are:*
Intention, Authenticity, Transparency.

*What **character words** could you add about yourself?*

1._____ 2. _____ 3. _____

*The **mentor/coach** I think of is Socrates.*

What mentor/coach do you think of? _____

Recommended Book:
The On Purpose Person by Kevin W. McCarthy

Commencements - Bill Gates
http://www.youtube.com/watch?v=AP5VIhbJwFs

After you watched the YouTube video, what inspired you?

Your thoughts: _____

2

Let's Get Started – You're Special

Go confidently in the direction of your dreams.
Live the life you have imagined.
--Henry David Thoreau

Felipe Ruiz Ricagni 1st

Executive Assistant & Programming/PR Coordinator at MundoFox

Los Angeles, California   Motion Pictures and Film

Current   MundoFox
Previous   Resolution Entertainment, Lionsgate, Retrofit Films
Education   Loyola Marymount University

Send a message   Endorse   ▾

403
connections

My Influencers: George Hess, Loyola Marymount University

Recently, an executive friend invited me to do a LinkedIn keynote training at a career night at a local church. About 45 people of all ages from all kinds of industries attended the event. At the beginning, the audience was wary of LinkedIn. By the end of the training, they eagerly asked questions and then gave me a standing ovation. After the meeting, I did a networking breakout to teach them how to interview for a job.

A few months later, by coincidence, I ran into my friend Chuck and asked him, "Do you know anybody who currently teaches at a college? I'm planning to write a book to help college students learn to effectively connect on LinkedIn and would love to get their input."

"As a matter of fact," he said, "remember that great career night you did? George Hess, a very good friend that I've known for 20 years, heard you speak. You should meet him. He has been a management professor at Loyola Marymount University for over 30 years."

"Wow, that's great," I said.

Chuck said, "He's involved in another church in Newport Beach that has a career workshop that meets every month. Why don't I introduce you as that marvelous speaker who did a great job for our people in transition?"

When I called George Hess, he was thrilled and asked how soon I could speak. I felt like I had just hit a home run.

I said, "I'd love to do the class. By the way, I hear you're a professor at LMU. Could you help me with my book for college students?"

"Chuck told me about your vision," he said, "and I'm thrilled. I think it's needed and can help our students learn how LinkedIn can introduce them to the people that could hire them."

I presented the workshop at his church and again got a standing ovation. People who had never heard of LinkedIn were excited to start their journey. The following month, Professor Hess invited me to give my talk to his management classes at Loyola Marymount University. I was delighted because these were exactly the students I wanted to reach. I delivered my talk to about 40 students, and then shared with them that I had a special offer for them. I invited them

---

*You never get a second chance
to make a first impression.*
Will Rogers

---

to a three-hour LinkedIn workshop training that I called my beta test for *Linkedin for College Students*. Working with the 12 students who attended, we built profiles for them and got them started on LinkedIn. His goal of being a producer was very congruent with path. They each understood the importance of connecting with others and building relationships that would benefit them as they finished their college days and entered the job force. In every industry, the top LinkedIn professionals show a bit of their culture in their profile picture.

My favorite example is my friend Felipe Ruiz Ricagni. When you look him up on LinkedIn, you will see that his picture could give us a thousand words about how he enjoys focusing on his work in the film industry. Felipe recently graduated from Loyola Marymount University in film and art with the goal of becoming a film producer. His picture shows him seeing a picture beyond a camera, which points him towards his goals in the industry.

CHINESE PROVERB
One picture is worth
ten thousand words

A Picture is worth a Thousand Words :)

This phrase is widely attributed to Frederick R. Barnard, who published an article, *One Look is Worth a Thousand Words*, in *Printer's Ink* in December 1921 on the effectiveness of graphics in advertising. He attributed the phrase to "a famous Japanese philosopher" although he later admitted he made up that origin and that he hired a calligrapher to put it into Chinese characters in the 1920s (see image below).

Even given this somewhat sordid history, the phrase does point out an important truth. The first forms of written language developed from a series of pictographs, first the ancient Egyptian hieroglyphics, then the cuneiform script of the ancient Sumerians. The ancient sailing merchants, the Phoenicians, then created the first known alphabet from these pictographic scripts.

Even before alphabets, ancient cave dwellers used images to convey important information with drawings of floods or men hunting mammoths on cave walls. Use of images has always been deeply entrenched in the human experience.

As time passed, the importance of the image to civilization has not changed and will never change. We as humans use our sight to make decisions about what to wear, what we will eat, where we will sleep, and who we will be attracted to.

This is why the images you use on LinkedIn are so important. If you have no picture, people may think less of you. If your picture is unprofessional, it might turn them off. A visitor will look at your picture and decide in 10 seconds if they want to know more about you. In those first 10 seconds, you must make your great impression that invites people to check you out.

Stephanie Mendiola   1st
Marketing Assistant at Mike Wolf Mastery
Hermosa Beach, California   Real Estate

Education   El Camino College

Send a message   Endorse   ▾   **256**
                                       connections

In networking and business you need to play the part. If you play golf with a business partner or meet a new client at the driving range, you don't wear a suit and tie, even if you are a finance industry professional who wears a suit and tie to the bank every day. On the golf course, you would wear a polo shirt and Bermuda shorts or a golf t-shirt and a pair of khakis. You wouldn't wear a suit to a rock concert on a Sunday night, but you would wear a suit to meet the Dean of Admissions when applying to medical school.

Many times you only have one instant to make a good impression on LinkedIn (and in life). How do you do that? You need a picture that fits as seamlessly into your profile as a window frame melds into a million dollar house. Your picture shows who you are in your industry. When your picture doesn't fit expectations, you give your viewers a sometimes unconscious sense of unease.

Not all people use a simple head shot. I've seen people in full baseball gear in their profile pictures to show they are a coach. Remember that this is only good in moderation. Too much creativity can give mixed signals to your viewers.

Always keep your photo as clean and simple as possible. The background in some pictures can be distracting. It is better to pose outside by a tree than use a fake generic background like a pretend beach with a beach ball, because truth creates the vibrations that attract people to us. Use a background that best represents your industry, but is not too busy.

You don't have to use a traditional studio and pay a lot of money to get a good portrait. Today's smart phones have high resolution cameras and make it easy to upload a profile picture in just seconds.

A great photo will include:
- A hairstyle that shows your face
- Clean, pressed, and appropriate clothes that fit the part
- A smile, one that appears as if you are looking at them though the camera lens.

The best advice I can give you is to look at hundreds of pictures on LinkedIn in the industry that you are considering.

When you upload a new picture, LinkedIn will share it with your connections. If you have several photos you like, switch them out every once in a while. You never know who might see your new photo and whether it might be the trigger that gets them to refer you to the person who is looking for someone just like you in your industry!

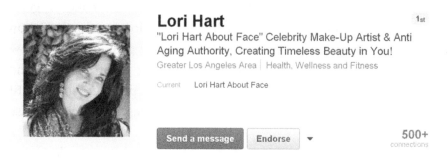

Lori Hart 1st

"Lori Hart About Face" Celebrity Make-Up Artist & Anti Aging Authority, Creating Timeless Beauty in You!

Greater Los Angeles Area | Health, Wellness and Fitness

Current   Lori Hart About Face

Send a message   Endorse   ▼   500+ connections

I met my friend Lori Hart at a three day video seminar. Everyone flocked to her energy. She has been coined "The Fairy Godmother of Beauty". We knew we would be instantly friends forever. What I love about Lori Hart is that she has the heart bigger than the ocean to help people feel and look beautiful because in her eyes, she sees our gorgeousness and inner beauty. Even though she has worked with many A list celebrities such as Eddie Murphy, Mariel Hemingway, Linda Gray plus many more...The tips Lori shares with my friends when they take pictures are, make sure you feel great, have your makeup and hair done in a natural fashion, vs. a glamour shot. When it comes to networking, feel confident. If you don't, ask as if! Don't be desperate. Remember you are the prize. You don't need a lot of money. Look clean, fresh, smile, feel great. Feel confident. A great attitude is the best. Ask questions of the people you are interviewing. Make it about them.

Your Story: Use your imagination like JK Rowling

"Imagination is more important than knowledge, for knowledge is limited to all we now know and understand, while imagination embraces the entire world, all there ever will be to know and understand," Albert Einstein said.

When it comes to your resume or your LinkedIn profile, you want to write like J.K. Rowling. *Harry Potter*, Rowling's most famous work, was all imagination. Use your imagination like she did.

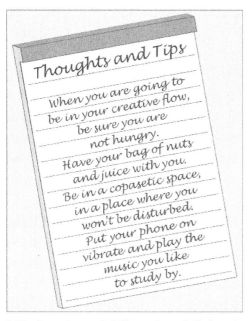

Thoughts and Tips

When you are going to be in your creative flow, be sure you are not hungry. Have your bag of nuts and juice with you. Be in a copasetic space, in a place where you won't be disturbed. Put your phone on vibrate and play the music you like to study by.

Rowling gave us the idea of calling a regular human a "Muggle" and wrote the novels from the perspective of wizards. Look at your resume on LinkedIn from the perspective of the wizards (your recruiters and connections). You don't want to be viewed as an ordinary "Muggle" but want to be chosen to receive on your 11th birthday, like Harry, the letter accepting you into Hogwarts School of Witchcraft and Wizardry. Lily's sister Petunia lived an ordinary lifestyle but Lily did not. Lily was accepted into Hogwarts while Petunia was not. Portray yourself as the person recruiters are looking for. Use words in your resume that draw recruiters to you.

Rowling created the amazing wizard Dumbledore, who could see through to who a person truly is. Dumbledore knew when he was just a student at Hogwarts that Tom Riddle was evil to his core. Many years later Tom became Voldemort. Dumbledore could read your LinkedIn Profile and see straight through to the real you. He could tell if your description is just pieces of your resume hashed into the LinkedIn Profile.

Not everyone is like Dumbledore. You must show who you truly are in your description of yourself. Your connections will not read between-the-lines because they are not Dumbledore. Present yourself as if you were trying to get Snape to see who you really are, not the pretentious person he considers you to be because he knows who your father is. Who you choose to be will convince the Sorting Hat to place you in Gryffindor and not in Slytherin.

> *Fairy tales are more than true; not because they tell us dragons exist, but because they tell us dragons can be beaten.*
> **Neil Gaiman**

Appearances can be deceiving, but they do matter. No one thought Neville Longbottom would become a hero. He appeared to be the dorky outcast who was never good at spells. In the end, Neville Longbottom stood up against Voldemort when everyone thought Harry was dead. Over time, we learned that the actor who portrayed Neville was a very handsome young man.

This story shows that appearances can be deceiving. In the beginning no one expected much from Neville but he surprised everyone when he turned the Boggart from Snape into Snape in his grandmother's clothes. Don't let your appearance make people believe in you less. Let your picture show who you are and what you can do. Appearances are everything, just as Snape was terrifying to Neville but became a person to laugh at in his grandmother's clothes. You can change the way others perceive you by changing your profile picture on LinkedIn.

Think of your connections as your wand. The wand chooses the wizard, according to Ollivander. Your connections choose you, but they don't do everything for you. The wand doesn't make the magic but is a channel for the magical spells to be made. Your connections are the same. Whether you choose your connections or they choose you, you need to master your connections to produce the end result you want. That end result is like severing a connection with the Avada Kadavra spell or lighting your way with a Lumos spell. If you don't use your connections, they will do nothing for you. If you learn

> *We keep moving forward opening new doors and doing new things, because we're curious and curiosity keeps leading us down new paths.*
> **Walt Disney**

to master the craft of connecting with people, they will carve a path for you in the darkness like a Lumos spell does.

SEO: What is it and how does it help you?

LinkedIn is your own personal mini-website. It gives you the opportunity to advertise yourself and connect with many people. To use it most effectively, you must pay attention to Search Engine Optimization.

Use your headline (or tagline) as your advertisement. This is a powerful key to getting recruiters, human relations representatives, and positive connections interested in you. The words in your headline are a billboard with keywords that attract people to you.

Keywords are gold. They are the words you want to be known by and known for. When you get clear on whom you are your words provide clarity about the job or position you are seeking. For maximum impact, use keywords that people are searching for.

John Chow is one of the top bloggers in the world. People don't look for him by name; they just want to find a blogger. It doesn't matter how many hits you get, it doesn't matter how many connections you have. It only matters what SEO words you use, because that is how the people you want to attract will find you. John Chow put every blog and writing word that you could think of in his header, his profile description, and his past experiences because that's how people will search for him.

Also use the current meaning of old words. For instance, content is the new word for writing, so recruiters looking for writers may search for content as well. You can also use other similar words such as writing, writer, and editor because some people might not search for content, but they might search for writing. In another field, instead of using market plans, I could use the word "launches." The goal is to hit some keywords people might embed in longer search phrases. If your simple keyword or two brings your profile up when a longer phrase is typed in, you will succeed in getting found.

LinkedIn Heading and Summary

 **Your Name**
Header: Add Keywords
Current: Jobs and Keywords
Previous: Jobs and Keywords

Summary Section:

Your name and tagline
Your email address and phone number
Your website address

Two blank rows

Your history,
no more than five lines

Two blank rows

Current story,
three lines

Two blank rows

Your specialties,
two lines

Two blank rows

► **P**roblem

One blank row

► **A**ction

One blank row

► **R**esults

Add a quote of yours and a call to action for people
to reach out to you.

To keep the attention of your connections, reword your header from time to time. When you edit your header, even just by a few words, the change shows up on the timeline of all your connections. That keeps you visible at the top of the search pages.

For keywords and SEO, find the words your future competitors use for their industry. As you work on your social media, spend 15 minutes to look at the profiles of these potential competitors. In each of the seven sections, the Heading, Summary, People also Viewed, Skills and Endorsements, Recommendations, Groups, and Companies They Follow, you will find the keywords they use. Make note of these words and use them as you create your LinkedIn profile.

Formatting: Start with the end in mind

The formatting in the Summary section is critical. You must create easy-to-read snippets that even a busy CFO will read. If the eye can't see the full picture, the visitor to your profile will flip to the next profile. Many things have changed with LinkedIn just like life evolves every day. In the beginning LinkedIn wanted people to put contact info in a designated section, but now it is common practice to put your name and information at the top of the summary. I like to make sure it is in this more prominent position at the top of the summary.

I have a dream that my four little children will one day live in a nation where they will not be judged by the color of their skin, but by the content of their character.

Martin Luther King, Jr.

Character isn't something you were born with and can't change, like your fingerprints. It's something you weren't born with and must take responsibility for forming.

Jim Rohn

Character and Skills = Home Run

Throughout this book, at the end of each chapter I will share my mentors and their characteristics. Here is a list of some character traits. Find five or six that express who you are. As you progress through the book, find other mentors and leaders and explore their traits. When it comes to great qualities in other people, as John Demartini says, "You can't see something in others that you don't see in yourself."

As we said in the "Who am I" section, you can use these character traits to reflect your skills in the specialties section and in your summary. Remember, some of these can be used again as your SEO keywords. Thread some of your character traits in your skills section.

Key Character Traits		
Accountable	Adaptable	Adventurous
Alert	Ambitious	Appropriate
Assertive	Astute	Attentive
Authentic	Aware	Bravery
Calm	Candid	Capable
Certain	Charismatic	Clear
Collaborative	Committed	Communicator
Compassion	Comradeship	Connected
Conscious	Considerate	Consistent
Contributes	Cooperative	Courageous
Creative	Curious	Dedicated
Determined	Diplomatic	Directive
Disciplined	Dynamic	Easygoing
Effective	Efficient	Empathetic
Empowers	Energetic	Enthusiastic
Ethical	Excited	Expressive
Facilitates	Fairness	Faithful
Fearless	Flexible	Friendly

Generative	Generosity	Gratitude
Happy	Hard Working	Honest
Honorable	Humorous	Imaginative
Immaculate	Independent	Initiates
Innovative	Inquiring	Integrates
Integrity	Intelligent	Intentional
Interested	Intimate	Joyful
Knowledgeable	Leading	Listener
Lively	Logical	Loving
Loyal	Manages Time Well	Networker
Nurturing	Open-Minded	Optimism
Organized	Patient	Peaceful
Planner	Playful	Poised
Polite	Powerful	Practical
Presents Self Well	Proactive	Problem Solver
Productive	Punctual	Reliable
Resourceful	Responsible	Self-confident
Self-generating	Self-reliant	Sense of Humor
Sensual	Serves Others	Sincere
Skillful	Spiritual	Spontaneous
Stable	Strong	Successful
Supportive	Tactful	Trusting
Trustworthy	Truthful	Versatile
Vibrant	Warm	Willing
Wise	Zealous	

Let's recap

*The **words of character** that resonate with me are:*
Creativity, Dreamer, Curiosity

*What **character words** could you add about yourself?*

1._____ 2. _____ 3. _____

*The **mentor/coach** I think of is Walt Disney.*

What mentor/coach do you think of? _____

Recommended Book:
The Messenger by Brendon Burchard

Commencements – J. K. Rowling
http://www.youtube.com/watch?v=wHGqp8lz36c

After you watched the YouTube video, what inspired you?

Your thoughts: _____

3

Click, Click, and Connect

Personal relationships are the fertile soil from which all advancement, all success, all achievement in real life grows.

-- Ben Stein

Deepak Chopra MD (official)   1st

Founder, Chopra Foundation

Greater San Diego Area   Health, Wellness and Fitness

Current   The Chopra Foundation, Deepak Chopra LLC, YouTube/The Chopra Well

Send a message   Endorse   ▾

500+
connections

My Influencers: Deepak Chopra

It was 20 years ago that I met Deepak Chopra. He was speaking at the Sutter Memorial Auditorium in Sacramento and I got the opportunity not only to hear him speak, but to actually meet him. If you do not know him, think Einstein mixed with Mother Teresa, a man who represents science crossed with metaphysics. More than that, he is a human being who walks in love, creativity, and gratitude. His most famous book is *Seven Spiritual Laws of Success*, published 20 years ago and still enjoyed by people of all ages. My favorite quote from this book is, "We are all one, and we are all connected in the universe." I love the work of Deepak Chopra and have been a fan for over 20 years.

Imagine my delight when while searching for new connections on LinkedIn I came across Deepak Chopra. You may be surprised to find that Deepak Chopra is on LinkedIn. I know I was. When I discovered this, I did my usual due diligence to get to know more about him. To my great delight, I found that Dr. Deepak Chopra had founded a group called *Collective Creativity*. The purpose of the group resonated with me. I applied to join it and was ecstatic when I was accepted. I am now connected with one of my favorite influencers, Deepak Chopra!

As you can see, there are many groups on LinkedIn that have great diversity in their interests and focus. Within those groups, you find people you consider "gold." Search for people and groups that resonate with you and align with your goals, visions, and aspirations.

Using Your Intuition: Sixth Sense Gut Instinct

Give whatever you are doing and whoever you are with the gift of your attention.
Jim Rohn

Deepak Chopra is well known for saying that we are all one with the universe and are connected to each other for a reason. I agree with Deepak and I do not believe that coincidences are simply coincidences. Everything that happens in life happens for a reason. Every person you meet is a person you were supposed to meet. Some of those people will become close relationships, others you will introduce to someone you know, and others you will forge business relationships with. All of them, everyone you meet, know, and come in contact with, can become part of your LinkedIn network. Use your intuition and be creative

U.C.B.
LIBRARY

when searching for connections. Some connections will jump right out. Others you will have to work to find.

Connecting on LinkedIn is similar to going to a networking event and collecting business cards. When you approach a stranger, you need to connect with them before they will give you their card. I forget the psychology behind this, but usually you meet somebody, you look in your partner's right eye, which is the eye on your left. This intuitive reaction helps build rapport with the person you have just met. If you don't connect, you won't get the card and you definitely won't get anywhere when you follow up to talk to them later. It's about the relationship, finding a connection between the two of you. This is where your Sixth Sense needs to be sharp. What do you have in common with the person you want to connect with? My connection with Deepak was creativity. Look at the person or their profile and read between the lines. Do you have the same classes or major? Did you come from the same state? Do you have similar hobbies? Using your intuition, find the piece of them that will best connect with a piece of you.

Once connected, you need to develop relationships with people. Relationships have to be managed and built over a period of time. Find a common bond or thread between you and build on that. It can be something silly, such as both of you love Lucy Ricardo and can sing the theme song to *Grease*. Even this small fact can start your relationship building.

For example, you might have a best friend you met in high school who you haven't seen in two years. You've been building this relationship for years. If this friend were to call you in the middle of the night, say he was stranded at the airport with no way to get home, and ask you to come get him, you would probably go and pick him up. That is how deep you want your relationships to be. Relationships need to be based on quality, feeling, and trust. Once built on a strong foundation, those relationships will help build your chances of getting the job you want after graduation.

You need to build 100 of these strong relationships. When you take time to build relationships in a strong manner, you will find all the connections you ever need. Maslow's law of building relationships with people states that you need a few basic things: air, water, food, sex, shelter, and significance. Everyone needs to feel significant in their lives. Connecting with people and giving them significance in your life allows you expand your relationships.

Making Connections Anywhere

I recently gave a keynote speech at a local church. When the event was over, several people approached me to tell me the speech inspired them. They had no idea you could develop a human connection using LinkedIn. One individual made me stop and think. This individual had been in transition for a while and all she said was, "You gave me hope." She gets it. My passion for LinkedIn is based on the connections you make, which might give you the answers you've been searching for, gain you an interview, or give you hope on a day you need it. You never know when the very next connection you make might open the door to the career you've sought.

People You May Know

You will find the "People You May Know" box on the right hand side of your home page. You can look at their profiles to see if you might want to connect with them. These possible connections are chosen for you by LinkedIn based on your profile and your other connections.

Who should I invite? Friends and Family?

Have you ever heard the term "fishbowl"? And no, I don't mean the bowl that your goldfish swim around in! Everyone has a fishbowl. Your fishbowl is your network of 10 to 100 friends and family members who like you, respect you, and support you.

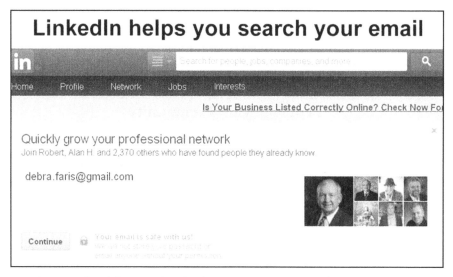

As you build your LinkedIn connections, make sure you build connections to your fishbowl, your 10 to 100 incredibly awesome people. One of the ways to do this is to find people they need to connect with. When you find such a connection, send it to them. They will open it and say, "Oh thank you!" It takes less than five seconds. It also takes less than five seconds to let your connections know you were thinking about them.

On each of your connections' profiles, next to the "Send a Message" button, you will find a bucket filled with actions you can take. One of them is "Share your Profile." If you find information on someone's profile that's beneficial to one of your connections, click the share button to send the profile to them. You can also use the button to follow up on someone you are not connected with yet but who you might want to connect with. These little bookmarks can make quite a difference for you.

Pieces to the Puzzle: "Memory Jogger"

For me a memory jogger is like pieces to a puzzle. We all have different ways to put a puzzle together. Most people turn all the pieces over and sometimes section them by color. Other people like to use the box as a guide and work from the outside in. When putting your list together, the memory jogger can help you find people that you know but that you wouldn't immediately consider for inclusion.

The Memory Jogger		
People in your Community		
Tax Person	Fireman	Church
Policeman	Insurance Agent	Dentist
Car Dealer	School Teacher	Dry Cleaner
Hair Dresser	Mechanic	Plumber
BabySitter/Daycare	Chiropractor	Gardener
Pediatrician/Doctor		
Sports		
Golf	Bowling	Water Sports
Hunting	Football	Tennis
Baseball/Softball	Basketball	
Hobbies		
Cooking	Book Club	Music
Hiking	Traveling	
Life Events		
Weddings	Birthdays	
Employment		
Summer Jobs	Internships	

Clubs and Groups		
Corporate Alliances	Tennis club	Fraternity
Academic Decathlon	Sorority	
Multi-Cultural Student Leaders	Honors Programs	Leadership
Best Buddies		
School Acquaintances		
Elementary	Junior High	High School
College	Yearbook	

Should I accept anyone? How many connections do I need?

In a way, yes, there is a magic number. And the magic number is 500. It's like a bad haircut. You don't want people to think you don't have enough. Your results on LinkedIn will only be as good as the quality and variety of the connections you develop. You might get more results with 200 very close connections that resonate with you than with 2,000 connections that are just names.

"Should I accept anyone who wants to connect?" The answer is simple. Think of accepting connections as like going to a party. You will find people you already know and are connected to. Then you'll meet people who form an instant connection with you. These are the people you know you like from the moment you start talking to them. Then you have the people that you don't connect with, don't like, and don't want to continue talking to. Your LinkedIn connections work the same way. Use your intuition to know whether or not this is someone that you want to have in your circle. If someone doesn't seem right for you and your career path, don't accept the invitation. If you like the person and want to get to know more about them and what they do, connect with them and begin the conversation. For some of you, accepting everyone will be fun and exciting as you build a huge network to draw on when the time comes. For others, your network may be more limited but more intimate, allowing in only those you're comfortable with and have built great relationships with. Both scenarios are effective. They work in different ways for different people.

One key question to ask is, "How much variety is there in my connections?" If you are self-employed, you might look for self-employed connections and pay attention to only the similarities between you and them. The smart person says, "I don't see the similarities between us, I see the differences." This is important because those differences mean that they have many connections you don't have. One of their connections might be a former CEO who could help with your job search.

Our first inclination is to look for those like us. Often as human beings, we stay inside our own circles and gravitate towards people who are similar to us. However, a richer and more satisfying experience is possible if we include our polar opposites in our circle. Think outside the box and connect with people whom you can help or can help you. If you want to show off your musical talents, connect with bands, orchestras, the entertainment industry, schools, anything you can think of where music is important. If sports are your entire life and you want to continue with it after college, look for connections in your sport, similar sports, broadcasting, teaching, refereeing, or vacation sports. Again, just like music, think outside the box and your possibilities will be endless.

When you connect with a person, always allow them to see all of your contacts, because that creates a measure of trust with the people you connect with. It's silly to hide your contacts, because that means you don't want to play the game. If you share your contacts and they're already in your fishbowl, your new connection may reciprocate and you may find people that will fit into your fishbowl among their contacts.

Let's recap

*The **words of character** that resonate with me are:*
Intuition, Connection, Relationships

*What **character words** could you add about yourself?*

1._____ 2. _____ 3. _____

*The **mentor/coach** I think of is Deepak Chopra.*

What mentor/coach do you think of? _____

Recommended Book:
The Seven Spiritual Laws of Success by Deepak Chopra

Commencements – Deepak Chopra
http://www.youtube.com/watch?v=P6gwFQ1pOPE

After you watched the YouTube video, what inspired you?

Your thoughts: _____

4

To Engage or Not to Engage

Think about what people are doing on Facebook today. They're keeping up with their friends and family, but they're also building an image and identity for themselves, which in a sense is their brand. They're connecting with the audience that they want to connect to.

-- Mark Zuckerberg

JONATHAN SPRINKLES   1st
Founder, GetAndStayMotivated.com
Houston, Texas Area   Professional Training & Coaching

Current   Sprinklisms Inc
Previous   Dell
Education   The University of Texas at Austin

Send a message   Endorse   ▾   **500+**
connections

My Influencers: Jonathan Sprinkles

Recently, I attended a great event that featured fabulous speakers in the college arena. One of these speakers, Jonathan Sprinkles, had recently been named College Speaker of the Year. While at the event, I took a quick break and out of 700 people attending the event there was not a soul in the hallway. As I returned to the seminar room, I looked up and saw this guy who I recognized as one of the keynote speakers. It took me a moment to figure out who he was. Suddenly, I realized he was Jonathan Sprinkles, the College Speaker of the Year. I reached my hand out and said, "Jonathan, I have heard so many wonderful things about you." He smiled at me and returned with a greeting of his own. At that moment I knew that he was part of my journey.

Who Viewed You?

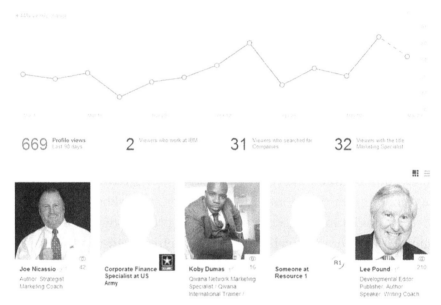

Do you remember the story of "The Tortoise and the Hare?" What about the phrase, "Slow and steady wins the race?" In both of these fables from childhood, the moral is that being persistent and taking things one step at a time will get you the results you desire. One of the 12 traits of over-achievers outlined in one of the most famous books in personal development history, *Think & Grow Rich* by Napoleon Hill, is to take small steps every day to accomplish your goals. The Tortoise who schedules five minutes every day will progress farther than the Hare who creates a burst of energy every few weeks. If you spend five minutes a day on LinkedIn, you will be like the early bird that gets the worm.

You meet people for a reason, much like I met Jonathan Sprinkles for a reason. Jonathan has an inspiring story that college students can relate to. He was failing in college until he read a book, *What Makes the Great, Great*, and decided to turn his life around and become a person of significance. You may also want to become a person of significance.

One of the most important tasks you can do in your five minutes a day is look at the five most recent persons to view your LinkedIn profile. This is a great advantage LinkedIn provides since no other websites give you that information. With this information, you can now view that person's profile and learn more about them.

First, look at how you are connected to them (if at all). Note the common traits, desires, and goals you share. Then look at what you do not share with this person. If you share nothing, there is always potential for you to be their polar opposite.

This person viewed you for a reason and that starts to forge a connection between the two of you, again for a reason. Even if you have nothing in common with this person, you should either send them an invite to connect or share their profile with someone you think would connect well with them. Helping other people today will make their tomorrow better and they will remember you in your future.

Who's in Your Fishbowl? Shared Connections

Earlier, I showed you how to identify the 10 to 100 most important people in your life. These are the people you invite to your wedding or who will attend your funeral, the people who are most visible in your life and in many cases the most likely to help you in time of need.

There is no such thing as a self-made man. You will reach your goals only with the help of others.
George Shinn

Although you want to develop and cultivate all of your LinkedIn connections, these 100 people may hold the key to your future. You need to build a connection with them at an emotional level, both one-on-one and in a group. People don't care about how much you know until they know how much you care. Spend time and energy fostering a strong relationship with these individuals. From there, you can build more distant connections and share your most important connections with people who would appreciate knowing them. It's important to share your connections with others and continue to foster strong relationships.

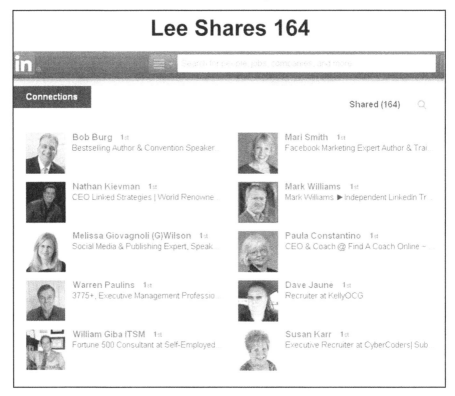

Sharing your connections is simple. When you find a connection that you know someone else can use, move your cursor to the right of the "Send InMail" button and right click; a drop down menu will appear, select "Share" and follow the steps. The person you are sending the connection to will get a LinkedIn "In Mail" with their profile attached. This is your opportunity to help those that are helping you.

What are Endorsements?

In the beginning, when LinkedIn brought endorsements to their platform, I had numerous calls from people confused as to what it was and why someone they didn't know was endorsing them. Some people find change difficult because they don't understand it. However, people who were used to Facebook were comfortable with the new addition to LinkedIn since it gave them an opportunity to have an online conversation by acknowledging something they liked about another profile, which they couldn't do anywhere else. I took a deep breath and realized that people's frustration came from a lack of understanding about the value of this new feature. One client I was working with was very confused. I explained to him that it was actually a compliment. The first question I asked was, "Did you look at your profile and search for the person's name and are they a first level connection?" Out of embarrassment but honesty, he acknowledged they were first connections.

I said, "Do you remember this person?"

Engage By Endorsements

After a moment's pause, he scanned the profile and said, "Oh, I remember him."

I asked, "Is there something in his profile that you like that could get the conversation rolling?"

> *Social media is changing the way we communicate and the way we are perceived, both positively and negatively. Every time you post a photo, or update your status, you are contributing to your own digital footprint and personal brand.*
> **Amy Jo Martin**

After looking at the profile, he found three things he liked and found a way to do business with the other party. When the ball bounces to your side of the court, it's your turn to give back. You can endorse a skill on his profile or take it one step deeper and send him a LinkedIn message. Within the week, he sent me a thank you back and said he was meeting his new LinkedIn friend in person.

When you notice a person who has over 99 endorsements, find the skill that's most endorsed on that profile that most resonates with you. Let's say its creativity. When you move your cursor to the right on the line where the photos are, it will show you everyone who has endorsed that person. It's fun to see who your first connections are but another opportunity to grow your LinkedIn connections is to look at level people who you can network with or who can help you build you path to an exciting job.

Positioning and Aligning

When you build your LinkedIn profile, it's important to use your character words with your skills in an alignment that is in harmony with your purpose and intentions. If you want to be a CFO and your profile shows that while in college you worked in the shipping department at Target, Walmart, or Home Depot but not in accounting, you will confuse those looking at your profile.

However, if you worked for the accounting department in Target, even in a very low position, you need to make that experience clear.

You position yourself when you find other LinkedIn members who do what you do or what you want to do and connect with them. This begins to build your well. When you're connected to someone who does what you want, other people will see you and you can move into their circles and connect with them.

Let's recap

*The **words of character** that resonate with me are:*
Innovation, Curiosity, Collaboration

*What **character words** could you add about yourself?*

1._____ 2. _____ 3. _____

*The **mentor/coach** I think of is Henry Ford.*

What mentor/coach do you think of? _____

Recommended Book:
The 7 Habits of Highly Successful People by Steven R.Covey

Commencements – Conan O'Brien
http://www.youtube.com/watch?v=KmDYXaaT9sA

After you watched the YouTube video, what inspired you?

Your thoughts: _____

5

Networking to the Next Level

One of the challenges in networking is everybody thinks it's making cold calls to strangers. Actually, it's the people who already have strong trust relationships with you, who know you're dedicated, smart, and a team player, who can help you.

-- Reid Hoffman

Bob Donnell   1st

Proven results strategist, taking entreprenuers, CEOs, celebrities and athletes to their Next Level

Orange County, California Area │ Professional Training & Coaching

Current   Next Level Live, Inc.

Education   School Of Life

Send a message ▼   500+
                                                  connections

My Influencers: Bob Donnell

Ever listen to those little nudges, those feelings that you need to meet a certain person? Not long ago, I was standing in a room filled with hundreds of people. Something inside me urged me to meet a man standing about a foot away, close enough to reach out and touch. I couldn't see his face, so I moved to catch a glimpse of his face, since I had no idea what he looked like or why I felt magnetized to meet him. Only his attire and stature told me he was a man. When I moved, he moved. I began to feel like a stalker. This little dance felt like it went on forever in that short moment of time.

I finally said, "Excuse me." He turned around and I smiled. He smiled back. I thought, "That was easy." I had no idea I had just met my match as a "Big Connector." Then I got extremely lucky and said something silly "like birds of a feather" and then asked, "Why are you here?" I was lucky because Bob is not a typical, "Hi, my name is… what is yours and what do you do?" networker.

I soon discovered that Bob Donnell is known for his program, "Connectology." His biggest No-No is to ask, "What do you do?" when you first meet another person. In Connectology, you learn that a person is far more than what they do. Finding out an occupation becomes a dead end in so many ways, particularly if you decide that they aren't in the field you are looking for. You never find out that they really are, you just create a superficial meet and greet. So many people get the quick occupational answer, reject it, and run off to the next person and the next person, only to find they are like a dog chasing its own tail.

In the first chapter, we discussed your "I am," the essence of who you really are. We discovered the character traits and the many gifts we possess that can lead us to untold opportunities as we journey down our career path. Adding new skills and degrees to those you have enables you to keep evolving and strengthening your own inner game to create a better you.

Here's the twist to networking. If you lead with the idea that you want to know more about the person you are meeting, you will create a higher quality relationship if you put the emphasis on them rather than yourself. Be present and truly interested in your new connection and you'll take that relationship to another level. In the book *Think and Grow Rich*, Napoleon Hill calls it 1 + 1 equals 3, a unique synergy which multiplies future possibilities instead of simply adding them together. When people know you as a connector, it enhances your credibility. It's not what you know, but who you know and who knows you!

Your Pitch: Are you in the Game or on the sidelines?

I never thought I needed a pitch when I met people. Then I attended an executive networking group that held a training class once a week. Part of the curriculum to train people who had lost their jobs (in transition) was how to create a pitch. Since I had been in the banking industry for 15 years and the banks were disintegrating, I figured I needed to check this class out. The curriculum taught students how to write a resume, have a mock interview, learn how to network, and to create a 30-second elevator Pitch. They taught that you need to know how to tell people in an instant in a clear and concise manner who you are and what you're looking for. It was a great way for me to sharpen my skills and acquire new ones.

Thoughts and Tips

Why them? What is their intention?

Be heart-centered, connect with them.

Voice is your instrument.

Eyes tell your sincerity.

Smile with kindness.

When I stepped into the class, it all seemed so natural for me that they were surprised with my natural unconventional networking manner. They were so impressed that they asked me to be one of the trainers. Two weeks later I stepped into the trainer position and two weeks after that they made me a lead trainer. It was cool being a trainer because I was helping people and at the same time honing my own skills.

One day I worked with a man in his 50s who had been a CFO (Chief Financial Officer) for over 25 years. He had only two jobs in his entire career, was making over a quarter million a year, and had been with the same company for over a dozen years. At the end of one day, I told the class that the next day we would give our 30-second pitch. As I handed him the assignment so he could prepare for the next day, he looked at me with a puzzled expression.

He showed up the next day and took his seat among the 14 people in the class. I put an example of a 120-word pitch up on the screen. "You need to present this pitch in 30 seconds or less," I said. His face reflected the look of an individual clearly apprehensive about taking on this task, but also determination to give it all he had. He had been a leader all his life, and this C-level executive wanted people to see him as a prospect for any job his new-found peers might know about. I saw hesitation. When his turn came, he stood and started to introduce himself but got so caught up in trying to remember the words that he stuttered and turned 50 shades of red. Did I say that this man was about 6'4" and weighed at least 220 pounds? I'm 5'3" and a little thing next to this big guy.

When the rubber meets the road you just jump in with both feet. I wanted him to know I would be his wingman and together we could do this. I stood next to him. His eyes were filled with tears. It broke my heart to see such a prideful man feel like he was a failure.

I remembered a Tony Robbins seminar I had attended where I learned about pattern interruptions. This would be the perfect time for me to share this technique with the class and make it fun at the same time. I told them, "Let's do the Hokey Pokey and turn ourselves around." They humored me and did the exercise as I instructed them. I could see the confusion on my CFO's face.

When we finished, I said, "Now, tell everyone what industry you are most interested in and tell everyone one thing that you could do to help them."

The man, now much more at ease, told everyone that he would be happy to help any of the class members by introducing them to any of his LinkedIn contacts. He then added that it would be an honor to do so and that his name was John Smith. He ended his 30-second pitch with, "Thank you very much. It's nice to meet all of you." The class jumped to their feet and gave him a standing ovation. It made me feel like I had made a huge difference for him.

In this situation, the man had shifted from thinking with his head to feeling with his heart. He functioned from a place of laughter and compassion.

When teaching you to create your own pitch, trainers will tell you, "Stand in front of the mirror and go blah, blah, blah." An even better option is to talk to a doll or teddy bear or the cutest thing you ever saw. When we talk to ourselves in the mirror we were talking from our heads. When we talk to another object, we are talking from our hearts. You shift into your being, your conversations, your body, and your caring. You come from laughter and compassion. You shift and your pitch shifts with you.

That's what has to happen on your LinkedIn. When you shift from being all about me to being all about what they need, everything shifts for you.

You also need to shift your conversations from your body to being and caring. On your LinkedIn profile, shift from thinking about yourself and what you can get out of a connection to thinking about what you can do for the other person. You will forge real connections where you will find true benefits. If you aren't thinking about whom your audience is, they may be repelled by what you have to say. If you pay attention to them, you will tailor the conversation that honors who they are. That will get you connections that matter.

F.O.R.M.

A lot of people ask me, "How do I network? How do I know who, when, where and how?" It is easy to figure this out, because people are attracted to like-minded people who share a common taste in things such as clothing, hobbies and careers.

When you understand this, you can learn to network any time anywhere. I learned this process in a network marketing company and it is still used all over the world in many companies. You can use it every day whether you are sitting in a dentist's office or you are networking at a social event. The "Who am I" who shows up is your integrity, your loyalty, your dependability, your creativity, all the human character traits that you bring to your networking.

The acronym for this process is F.O.R.M.

- F is for where they are From. I also like to ask where they were born. I have found that many people have known their friends for many years but never knew whether these friends came from a place they had in common or had a place they always wanted to explore.
- O is for your Occupation. Asking a new connection what industry they work in is important both for someone who is in transition or someone who already works for a company.
- R is your Recreation. A lot of people like to talk about their hobbies and what they do on weekends.
- M is your Message. Your message is how you can help potential employers when you are looking for a job.

From: You ask your new connection two questions, "Where are you from?" and "Where were you born?" You wait for the answers, take two seconds to pause. After you give your connection the opportunity to share where they are from, reflect back to them where you were born and where you live. You may discover you have something in common.

Occupation: What do you do or what industry are you in? Remember, if your connection is in transition and the networking event is about job-hunting, stick to mentioning your industry and don't add who you work for. Reflect back to them the parts of your career that complement their past or present career.

Recreation: You may meet someone at a social gathering or fun event. It is easy to start a conversation about the hobbies, sports, or other fun things. Reflect commonalities between you, which will build a bond as each of you discovers more about the other.

Message: Now that you have established rapport, you can share that you are on LinkedIn and would be happy to help them with some of your connections. Ask yourself, "What is the one key thing that I could ask if they need help with."

Qualify like a CEO

As a college student, you are not yet in the work world. However, you may have many opportunities, particularly in extra-curricular activities, to help another student get a position he wants. Here is an example from the professional world.

Let's say you have become a CFO who works in Los Angeles but you commute 50 miles from Orange County and you would like to find a job closer to home in Orange County.

If you're not making mistakes, then you're not doing anything. I'm positive that a doer makes mistakes.
John Wooden

One ideal way to make that happen is find a referring partner. First you go to LinkedIn and find a CFO that's in transition and ask him to visit you in Orange County. You sit down for breakfast or lunch with this partner and say, "You're a CFO and I'm a CFO and my wife would be very unhappy if we moved out of Orange County because our kids and our church are here. I know that you want to work in Los Angeles and I want to work in Orange County. How about sharing leads? I can give you leads I hear about in Los Angeles and you can share Orange County leads with me."

Remember that even in college, people are people and have needs that they have to take care of. If you eliminate the fear that you might take away another person or student's position, you now have as a partner a 100% invested person that has the same goal as you. Working together and networking in your respective areas, you can help each other be successful.

Networking Tips

- Keep your body language open if you want to get to know someone. Hold your shoulders a little bit back. When you shake their hand, look them in the eye.

- When you are at a networking event where you want to meet people, everybody has a comfort zone. If you sense you are too close based on the other person's reaction, step back. They are telling you that you are in their space. It's nothing to be offended over, just give them more space.

- Networking is about getting out of your head and into your heart.

- People need to feel comfortable with who you are and how you show up.

- When you network, you have to change hats depending on your audience. You wouldn't talk in a business office like you would talk at a baseball game. You have to think from your audience's perspective.

- When you smile, you show another of your human sides and people will feel comfortable with you.

- Remember to keep your questions light. People don't like to feel that they are being interrogated.

- Keep your conversations and your body in a caring posture. Come from laughter and compassion.

- Sometimes we can give too much information about ourselves and then people make judgments.

- When all else fails and you don't know who to talk to, look for the guy or gal who is standing alone and seems to be thinking, "Why am I here?" He knows why he's there. He just doesn't know how to approach other people. So be the hero and start conversations with F.O.R.M.

What is Left-Brain Right-Brain connecting?

I'm sure you've heard the terms "Left-Brained" and "Right-Brained" before, but have you ever considered the depth of the terms' meaning? A Left-Brained individual is a person who utilizes mostly the left side of their brain, making that individual more analytical, logical, and objective. A Right-Brained individual uses mostly the right side of their brain, which leads to a more subjective, thoughtful, and intuitive approach.

Left-Brain dominant individuals typically fill roles such as CFO (Chief Financial Officer) and COO (Chief Operating Officer) due to their analytical capabilities. Right-Brain dominant individuals typically fill roles such as CMO (Chief Marketing Officer), CNO (Chief Networking Officer) and CEO (Chief Executive Officer), although these people can fall into either category depending on whether they were appointed or founded the company.

When I work with C-level Left-Brained dominant individuals who love equations and analytics, I find that trying to get them to do anything creative or unorthodox makes them uncomfortable. When I work with the Right-Brained dominant individuals, who love creativity, they get lost in the massive amount of information analytics provides. It dawned on me that the perfect pairing was to match Left-Brained and Right-Brained persons, who will then complement each other perfectly and produce both the analysis and the creativity that successful companies and people require.

This concept also works when two opposite individuals work together on LinkedIn. The "Right-Brain" dominant person can create a more attractive profile while the "Left-Brained" dominant individual can create more detailed content and catch errors that are not obvious. When two people from opposite sides of the coin get together, they will produce a more balanced and robust LinkedIn profile. This pertains to writing a profile and also works amazingly well in person when connecting with another human being.

A Left-Brained individual may stand in a corner and analyze the room. They might come from a place of judgment versus the place of observation the Right-Brained individual prefers. Each will communicate in different styles and operate in different styles. Yet when they work together, they complement each other and help each other by introducing new contacts they could not have discovered alone. This is a great way to network since the Left-Brained individual is good with detail and can be a great accountability partner for the Right-Brained individual. Each individual will open doors for the other, creating a perfectly balanced networking team.

Try this out by meeting at least three people who are your opposites the next time you go to a networking event. If you are an extrovert, look for someone who is more introverted. If you are creative, look for a good organizer. If you think you are introverted and not a networker, look for the friendliest person in the room and start a conversation. You will meet your exact opposite, the very person you need to meet, because when the two of you come together you never know what might happen.

Go Deep in Your Connections

In the book *Think and Grow Rich*, Napoleon Hill tells the story of R. U. Darby, a Maryland businessman who discovered a rich vein of gold in the Colorado Mountains. They followed the vein until it gave out. Certain that no more gold existed, they quit and sold out to a junk dealer, who found a new vein of gold just three feet away from where Darby had stopped. The junk man made millions. So I want to share with you, many people give up when they are only three feet away!

In social media it is a common to hear people say "Six Degrees to Kevin Bacon" phrase, because people realized that through this person they could ask someone do you know someone who knows Kevin Bacon and then they would continue to ask so on and so forth. In theory, this means everyone in the world is connected to everyone else in the world by a chain of no more than six people. This was shown in the movie, *Six Degrees of Separation* with Kevin

Bacon. With LinkedIn I have found people with three or four searches. The closer the alignment the closer you are to finding them.

The Deeper You Go, the Closer You Get to Gold

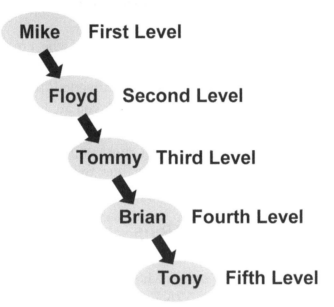

With a few searches on LinkedIn, you can find almost anyone you want to connect with because LinkedIn can link you to 300 million of the billions of people on our planet.

Network like a Rockstar

We like to be with people like us and this one was easy for me. At an event and I heard someone say, "I teach networking at colleges." I wiggled my way next to him through a swarm of people around him. "We should talk," I said. "I want to know more about you and your mission." He said he's focused speaking at MBA programs at Harvard, Stanford, Columbia, Cornell, and UPenn.

Jaymin Patel 1st

Author/Speaker/Coach - "The Rockstar Career Guy" that inspires students and professionals about college and career!

Greater New York City Area | Professional Training & Coaching

Current	The MBA Guide to Networking Like a Rockstar, Exploration Impact Publishing, LLC
Previous	Booz & Company, General Mills
Education	Carnegie Mellon University

Send a message Endorse ▼ 500+ connections

Jaymin Patel says it's simple. When a recruiter or an influential individual meets they will mentally place you in one of four buckets: Yes. No. Maybe. Or ROCKSTAR!

The key to coming across as a Rockstar, he says, is to use confidence and communication skills (both are skills that can be learned!) to stand out from the crowd and building *personal relationships* with influential individuals. The key includes having a range of diversity within your network.

For example, if you are a Liberal Arts major, it's important to develop relationships with individuals who are in other disciplines who have different values and perspectives, such as Accounting or Engineering. This diversity in networks is beneficial for a variety of reasons:

1. It enables you to be a connector who can bring two usually separate groups of people together.
2. It allows you to be more self-aware and open-minded by understanding a diversity of viewpoints
3. It exposes you to opportunities that you may not be aware of

"It's not always easy to build a relationship with a person who is different from you," says. "However, it's easier than you might think. Use use my Three Word Intro, which goes like this: 'Hi, I'm Jaymin.'"

> *Who are the top 10 most powerful connections you have? The people who can make things happen for you! Then ask yourself, what have I done for these people lately? Or, maybe a better question is, are these people you just call every once in a while to suck their blood.*
> **Jeffrey Gitomer**

This approach works 99% of the time, he says. "When the other person does not respond that's ok. Just use the Three Word Intro on the next person! For best results, use it in an environment common to the individual you are speaking with, such as in the classroom, at a local museum, or anywhere on campus."

Once Jaymin used the Three Word Intro on a plane. That stranger became one of the most impactful individuals in his career. "He connected me with an opportunity I wasn't aware of," he said. "I left my full-time job and became an author, speaker, and coach reaching thousands around the world."

He added, "When you know how to start a conversation with anyone, you can build diversity into your network by networking like a ROCKSTAR!"

Relationship Currency

Relationship Currency is such an interesting topic. When he speaks about relationship bank accounts Steven Covey says "First seek to understand then to be understood." If you had an account that had $1,000 and all you did was take money out and never to make any deposits, it wouldn't be too long before it was empty. There used to be a saying save your pennies for a rainy day (now it would be dollars). However there are some people who will ask again and again for things and we may feel like they never give anything in return. The same goes on in networking and on LinkedIn. People will ask for a recommendation and they have never even made another point of communication after the initial invite, not alone a phone call but they want you to recommend them? It's kind of confusing especially when you are new and you want to build someone relationships. So how do you build your own LinkedIn currency? Here are a few tips:

1. Looking through your new updates and when you see one of your new connections got a job, send them congratulations.

2. Someone has a new photo, tell them you noticed.

3. You see a new member in a group, go look at their profile and then send them a welcome to the group with a nice comment about their profile and send them a welcome with a nice comment

4. When you see a job that is in the industry of one of your top 20 send them the Link of forward them the job posting.

5. When you see a charity on one of your friend's profiles, ask them more about it.

Jill Lublin   1st
Master Publicity Strategist, Speaker & Author -
Promising Promotion and Management Consulting
San Francisco Bay Area   Management Consulting

Current   Promising Promotion
Education   Wayne State University

Send a message   Endorse   ▼   500+
                                             connections

How to Win Friends and Influence People

Sometimes life comes full circle. One of the very first leadership training courses I took was Dale Carnegie. At the time I didn't know Mr. Carnegie had passed before I was born. The core values and principles he taught are timeless. Many years later in Vegas, I attended Author 101 heard Jill Lublin, author of the best seller *Networking Magic* speak.

Later that afternoon I bumped into her in the hall, had a nice chat, and exchanged cards, just enjoying our moment together and connecting. I thanked her for her words of wisdom.

Later I looked her up on LinkedIn and discovered she was a modern-day Dale Carnegie on how to be influential. She's been featured in the New York Times, Women's Day, Fortune, Small

Business, Inc., and Entrepreneur Magazine, and on ABC, CBS, NBC TV and radio. When your values align with other great peoples values it creates a strong foundation for new relationships.

Here's one of Jill's tried and true philosophies:

*Without introductions, matches can't be made.

*Without matches, connections cannot be created.

*Without connections, bonds cannot form

*Without bonding, relationships cannot be built and

*Without reciprocal relationships, networks cannot last

Continue to grow your friendships to the next level.

Let's recap

*The **words of character** that resonate with me are:
Synchronicity, Optimism, Strategy*

*What **character words** could you add about yourself?*

1._____ 2._____ 3._____

*The **mentor/coach** I think of is John Wooden.*

What mentor/coach do you think of? _____

Recommended Book:
Never Eat Alone by Ken Frazzi

Commencements – Barbara Kingsolver
http://www.youtube.com/watch?v=i5YxR9B0VAQ

After you watched the YouTube video, what inspired you?

Your thoughts: _____

6

Groups, Tribes, and Communities

What tribes are is a very simple concept that goes back 50 million years. It's about leading and connecting people and ideas. And it's something that people have wanted forever.

-- Seth Godin

JD GERSHBEIN   1st

THE NEUROSCIENCE OF LINKEDIN ♦ SOCIAL
BRANDING for LinkedIn Profiles ♦ SPEAKER &
CONSULTANT on LinkedIn Best Practices

Greater Chicago Area   Online Media

Current   THE LINKEDIN EDGE: Creating a Psychological Advantage in
           Social Business, The Huffington Post, OWLISH
           COMMUNICATIONS

Previous   NBC Inc.Well, CARTOONS THAT MEAN BUSINESS™

Education Illinois Institute of Technology (Stuart Graduate School of
           Business)

Send a message   Endorse   ▼   500+
                                           connections

My Influencers: J. D. Gershbein

Although I did not meet JD Gershbein in a LinkedIn group, this area has special significance to me when I think of him. JD is one of the true influencers on LinkedIn. He does not need to state this fact. It becomes obvious when you read his writing, speak with him, or watch what he does on LinkedIn. JD is the real deal when it comes to guiding others and giving them the Aha moment. In getting to know JD, he walks his walk and talks his talk authentically and transparently. His genuine love for teaching others oozes from everything he shares, and enjoy is human touch when it comes to engaging the LinkedIn community. He is also an adjunct professor of marketing communications at the IIT Stuart School of Business in his hometown of Chicago, teaching social media marketing to MBA candidates. But it is how I learned of JD, and got to know him, that is the real story here.

> *It's always been a great survival value for people to believe they belong to a superior tribe. That's just in human relationships.*
> **E. O. Wilson**

One day, I was surfing LinkedIn and JD popped up. I went through my regular process of checking people out online, and before I knew it, I was riveted by his videos, company profile, work history, websites, and, yes, his LinkedIn groups. Although JD is a LinkedIn consultant and coach, I did not sense that he was my competitor. Instead, I saw our commonalities and how we would complement each other. I decided on the spot that I would make an effort to reach out to JD. Knowing that we only have one chance to make a first impression, I did my homework on him, took a deep breath, and wrote an invitation to connect on LinkedIn that was as sincere and personal as could be. I told him that I could help him get known on the West Coast. I even included my cell phone number. I was extending out the ol' olive branch, pushing for an offline conversation.

To my surprise and pleasure, JD not only graciously accepted my invitation, but came back with a beautiful message. He thanked me for inviting him, and told me that I was welcome to call him anytime. When we eventually connected on the phone, it was like I had known this guy all of my life. I felt like I had a combination of Albert Einstein and Walt Disney, with a little Seth Godin thrown in for good measure on the other end of the phone. (Seth is another hero of mine. JD, if you don't know, looks a lot like Seth. We both feel he is one of the best writers out there on business culture.) JD's intelligence, eloquence, and humorous way of telling stories captivated me from the get-go. Our initial call went well over an hour.

As the frequency of our conversations increased, I learned that JD shared my opinions about LinkedIn groups. We both acknowledge them as essential to one's overall success on LinkedIn. JD is a shining example of how to get your voice heard on LinkedIn. Being active in the groups gets you noticed and can ultimately grow your network and bring more opportunities. I have my own LinkedIn group, more than 1,000 members, where people can take their on-line connections off-line, meet them face-to-face, and build higher quality relationships. Through my association with JD, I have learned how to be a better group manager. I recommend that college students explore the LinkedIn groups, join the ones they find most interesting, and learn as much as they can about the people in them.

What we have to do is to find a way to celebrate our diversity and debate our differences without fracturing our communities.
Hillary Clinton

JD manages the Linked Strategies group, the preeminent community for exchanging ideas about how to use LinkedIn most effectively. People who join this group are LinkedIn consultants, coaches, digital marketers, and anyone interested in taking the deep dive on LinkedIn. This is an example of a group that is focused on a single area. JD helps keep the many discussions on track and makes sure that people in the group support their fellow members. When it comes to showing others to how to build communities and make people feel special in them, JD Gershbein is one to follow.

I affectionately call JD "my brother from another mother." I talk about him as being left brain, me being right brain, although I know JD has an ample supply of each side. He is funny, witty, and incredibly smart and has a heart of gold. We have talked about collaborating for a long time, and I know that we will make it happen someday. The lesson here is to be bold. When you feel strongly about connecting with someone, just do it! Such is the power of LinkedIn.

Seven Ways to Pick a Group

Do you remember back in grade school when the kids picked teams for kickball? You never wanted to be the last one picked. How about tryouts for football or cheerleading in high school? Waiting hours after the last practice to see if you made the team was agonizing; and even worse if you found out you'd been cut. And then there are college acceptance letters. I remember waiting by the mailbox day after day to see if mine had arrived. Being part of the right group has always been an important part of our identity and is an important part of LinkedIn as well. Being associated with the right group can help you land the right job!

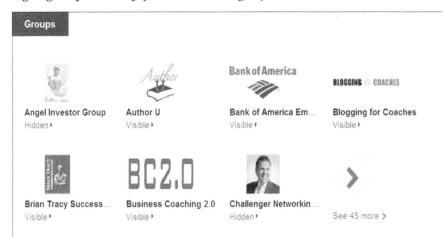

If you look at Mike Ferry™'s LinkedIn page, you will see that he has joined a lot of groups that include realtors. This makes a lot of sense if, like Mike, you are one of the top real estate professional trainers in the world. However, it makes no sense at all if you are a real estate agent. Many agents make a huge mistake when they create their LinkedIn profiles. They join groups made up of other realtors. They think that by being visible in the realtor community, they will attract customers. What is the mistake? When you do this, other realtors will find you and look at your profile. Nobody else will. The most important question you can ask yourself, the question that means everything for you and your business, is, "Is a realtor going to sell a house to another realtor?" Rephrase this question so it applies to your business.

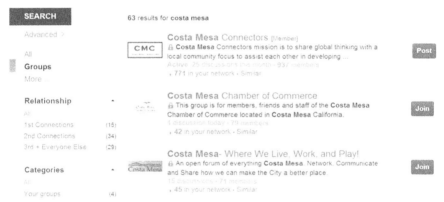

Searching for groups is very simple on LinkedIn. The search bar allows you the find People, Updates, Jobs, Companies, your Inbox, or Groups. You want to make Groups your default. Just change your settings.

LinkedIn is home to over 2,000,000 groups. Groups representing every industry, hobby, life interest and passion can be found on LinkedIn. Picking a group is like picking music. With so many genres available, it is critical that you chose the ones that fit your purpose in your profession but also in your personality and gifts. Here are some options:

1. **Group Size - Papa Bear, Mama Bear, and Baby Bear:** (this is a fun metaphor that I use to remember group size)
   a. The first thing you want to select when you are picking a group is to pick a huge group, the Papa Bear
   b. Then pick a medium-sized group, the Mama Bear
2. Then add a small group, the Baby Bear
3. **Fun-Fun-Fun**: Of the 2,000,000 groups on LinkedIn, pick a fun, exciting group that makes you think, "Wow, if I could do this for a living, this would be fun."
4. **Recruit Me. I want a job**: Find out where all the Human Resources people, recruiters and headhunters play. Seek them out and speak to them.
5. **People like Me**: Find groups with people like you that you can ask, "What works for you and what doesn't."

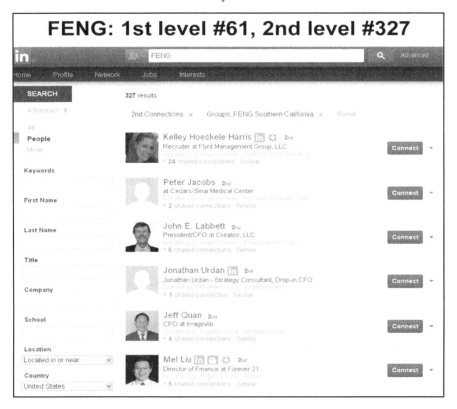

6. **Who are your Top 25**? Look at their groups and join groups that make sense for you.

7. **Job Groups, Headhunters, and Recruiters:** Joining these groups is the key to successful searches for recruiters who live in your community or are recruiters for your industry or field

8. **Top Link**: I have saved the Best for Last. This open Networkers Group (TopLink.com) has 138,000 members. If you are not yet a member, you can click the "Join Group" button. This open networkers group includes some of the very largest connectors on LinkedIn, many of whom have many thousands of connections. When you first join this group, let the Open Networkers Logo show up on your profile since it might attract more connections interested in what you do. In the future, however, when you reach a higher level on LinkedIn and want to show only high quality groups in your profile, do not show the TopLink Logo because it means that you're an open connector. If want to keep your connections more private and want them to look at you as a careful connector with special people, you don't want them to know you are an open networker.

Do make it a practice to explore the many groups on LinkedIn. Before you join any group, you can see the members of the group who are in your network and in some groups you can read discussion threads. At the very least, you can see who the group owner is, how many members the group has, and whether it is open or closed. Once you join, you can see the other people who belong to the group

When you see the five or six connections of yours that are members of the new group, you might think, "Oh my goodness, all of these people are first connections with me. These individuals have (for instance) painting careers but I'm not in this group with them." If you see that six of your first level connections are in this art group and you are interested in art, you might want to pursue stronger connections with those people."

You do want to join the maximum of 50 groups because when you are in a group, you can send emails to all the members of a group without being connected to them. This opens up hundreds of thousands of people who can send you a message. However, work just the top three of these groups strongly so you do not make extra work for yourself. Work smarter, not harder.

What's a tribe and who are your key players?

In order to effect great change, we need to look at how we can help those in our own communities as well as globally.
Christina Aguilera

If you look up the word "tribe" in the dictionary you will get this definition: a social division in a traditional society consisting of families or communities linked by social, economic, religious, or blood ties, with a common culture and dialect, typically having a recognized leader.

Your most important job on LinkedIn is to find others in your field. Begin by looking at 100 people who do what you do on LinkedIn. You will see how they target their tribe and you will find good connections who could refer business to you. I've looked at thousands of profiles, so I have a good idea what a successful profile contains. If you haven't looked at your first 100 people, then you have no idea who is out there and who can help you.

Keep a notebook labeled *Tips and Ideas for LinkedIn*. When you find people who might be good connections, make a note of them. Write down how that person resonates with you and what that person might mean to you. Then connect with them.

When you do connect with your new contacts, the most critical thing you can do is acknowledge them. Before you connect, the button beside the profile picture says, "Connect." After you connect, it says, "Send a message." When I connect with another person, one of the key things I do is click that button and send them a message thanking them for connecting with me. This is the best way to build relationships on LinkedIn and it takes just 60 seconds.

Group Etiquette and Settings

Did your grandma ever tell you to take your elbows off the table? How about which fork to use to eat the salad? And how many times have you been told not to talk with your mouth full? These are all forms of etiquette. Believe it or not, forms of etiquette exist in dealing with groups on LinkedIn as well. Many realtors will jump into just realtor groups. Job seekers do the same thing. They jump into every Job group they can find.

When a visitor looks at your profile and sees groups focused on job seekers, they think that if they reach out to you, all you will want from them is a job.

One time I was in a real estate office talking with a friend and another person walked in the door. All of a sudden 30 agents in the office picked up the phone.

I said to my friend, "What the heck was that? I just saw 90% of the agents grab the phone and stick it to their ear."

Social media is not about the exploitation of technology but service to community.
Simon Mainwaring

My friend laughed and said, "Yeah, that man who walked in is a title company representative. The agents put the phone to their ear so the title person wouldn't stop at their desk to talk to them. It is their way of avoiding telling him they are too busy to talk."

The same thing can happen on LinkedIn. When you put the wrong group logos on your profile, many people will not want to connect with or talk to you. The best way to avoid this is to hide the group logos that aren't attractive to your viewers.

When you set up your group membership settings, make sure to unclick two items, your logo for the groups you don't want others to see and your digest, unless the group is one of your top three, in which case you want to get every message everybody is sending because this is your tribe. You don't want every message from the other 49 groups. Unclick the daily digest if you don't want to get daily or weekly messages. However, always click the bottom two buttons which allow the Group Manager to send you email and other members to send you messages.

For digest emails, you have a choice of weekly or daily emails. A very busy person will unclick both of those for all but a few groups. You can change the settings from a daily notice to a weekly notice if you prefer. For groups where there is too much chatter, don't allow digest messages.

My Parents and Other Baby Boomers

For college students, it is good to know what groups your parents have joined. Why? It's pretty good chance that the person in HR, the person who is going to hire you, and the person who gave the person the authority to hire you are all older than you. Why not know where they hide out and who they communicate with? Don't forget to your get your parent's connections and add them to your LinkedIn

There's a common saying, "It's not what you know, it's who you know." That statement has a lot of value, but there is an even better one: "It's not who you know, but who knows you." When I started studying LinkedIn, I realized there is an even more powerful level of connection, "It's not who you know, but who they know!"

The best memory jogger is your parents. I know it seems silly because you're finally out on your own. However, your parents have years and years of relationship currency with people who know people, like the Kevin Bacon's six degrees. Those people could introduce you to the HR person or the recruiter for the very company you want to work for.

Generation Y – Millennial's Favorite groups

Young Entrepreneur

Young Entrepreneur Connections
This group is designed to benefit all **young** entrepreneurs. Tech, health, web, finance, sales, marketing etc. if you are a ...
Very Active: 212 discussions this month   6,487 members
▸ 816 in your network   Similar

Young Social Entrepreneur (YSE) Group - 'Say 'YES' to Social Enterprise
Young Social Entrepreneurs unite. A place to share, teach, discuss and learn. A triple bottom...
Active: 27 discussions this month   1,202 members
▸ 149 in your network   Similar

Conceptua :: Young Professional & Entrepreneur Networking
Provide a unique and fresh approach to networking by focusing on opportunities and social capital for the **young** ...
133 discussions   380 members
▸ 69 in your network   Similar

Young Entrepreneur in Mauritius
All **young entrepreneur** in Mauritius together to share ideas
8 discussions this month   367 members
▸ 10 in your network   Similar

Young Entrepreneur Network of BYU
▪ The Associate **Entrepreneur** Network of BYU Alumni is a group of recent graduates interested in meeting like-minded ...
37 discussions   330 members
▸ 91 in your network   Similar

Young Professional

Texas Young Professionals (Houston, Dallas, San Antonio, Austin & Fort Worth Chapters)

🔒 Texas Young Professionals is a community of young... relationships with other young professionals...

Very Active: 183 discussions this month · 56,059 members

, 7,829 in your network · Similar

Detroit Young Professionals (DYP)

🔒 Detroit Young Professionals (DYP) is a nonprofit organization that provides professional development, social networking ...

Very Active: 94 discussions this month · 17,711 members

, 1,966 in your network · Similar

NetParty - Business and Social Networking Events for Young Professionals

🔒 The Worldwide Young Professionals Network. Over 200,000 young professionals have registered at NetParty.com! As seen in ...

544 discussions · 24,982 members

, 4,569 in your network · Similar

College

University of Maryland, College Park Alumni Association (Official)

🔒 This University of Maryland, College Park Alumni Association group serves to expand our network of connections, ideas, and...

Active: 27 discussions this month · 25,677 members

, 2,679 in your network · Similar

Entry Level Jobs and Internships: College Recruiter

A LinkedIn group for corporate recruiters, college recruiters, and career services professionals with a focus on ...

Very Active: 137 discussions this month · 22,750 members

, 1,508 in your network · Similar

Boston College Alumni Group

🔒 One of the largest & most active University alumni groups on LinkedIn with over 20,000 members. This group is set up ...

Active: 25 discussions this month · 25,577 members

, 2,020 in your network · Similar

Students

Students and Recent Grads [Official]

Welcome to the official LinkedIn Guide for **Students** and Recent Grads. The goal of this group is to support current **students** ...

Very Active 432 discussions this month   62,785 members

▸ **3,855** in your network   Similar

The Official Brigham Young University (BYU) Alumni Network, Current **Students** Welcome

Brigham Young University encourages its alumni to connect to each other worldwide, building lifelong relationships and ...

11 discussions this month   38,513 members

▸ **4,264** in your network   Similar

Texas Exes - The University of Texas Ex-**Students'** Association

The official LinkedIn group of the Texas Exes, the alumni association of The University of Texas at Austin. To join, you ...

Very Active 71 discussions this month   45,146 members

▸ **4,585** in your network   Similar

Generation Y

Generation Y

Gen **Y** is all about sharing ideas about Gen **Y** and the impact **Generation** Y is making in the workplace and in the consumer ...

Active 26 discussions this month   1,459 members

▸ **268** in your network   Similar

Millenials or **Generation Y**

Being a millenial myself, I find it interesting how the baby boomers and **generation** X and ourselves are so different in ...

1 discussion this month   233 members

▸ **40** in your network   Similar

Generation Y Leadership Network

The **Generation** Y Leadership Network is intended for young, ambitious leaders who often work in an project driven ...

1 discussion this month   165 members

▸ **12** in your network   Similar

Millenials

Millenials or Generation Y
Being a millenial myself, I find it interesting how the baby boomers and generation X and ourselves are so different in ...
1 discussion this month · 233 members
40 in your network · Similar

Social Business Strategies & Discussion Forum - Enterprise
Social Business Strategies and Discussion Forum is an invitation only forum for enterprise class corporations. This forum...
14 discussions this month · 41 members
14 in your network · Similar

Mekanism Millenials [Subgroup]
Mekanism Networks - Influencers Reaching Millenials
1 member
Similar

The Next Generation

Nuclear Power - the next generation
This group is for those interested in new nuclear power plants, nuclear energy, and issues associated with the nuclear ...
Very Active · 193 discussions this month · 29,650 members
2,012 in your network · Similar

Brandixit | The Next Generation Branding Community
Brandixit The next generation branding community
Very Active · 180 discussions this month · 16,502 members
2,648 in your network · Similar

Alumni

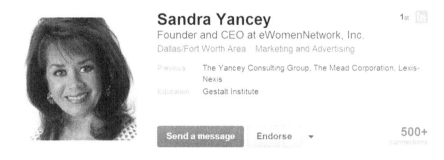

Sandra Yancey
Founder and CEO at eWomenNetwork, Inc.
Dallas/Fort Worth Area   Marketing and Advertising

Previous   The Yancey Consulting Group, The Mead Corporation, Lexis-Nexis
Education   Gestalt Institute

Send a message   Endorse   ▾

500+
connections

1st

Follow a Leader - Be a Leader

Have you ever stopped at a long traffic light only to notice that there are far fewer cars in the lane next to you? The next time you stop at a light, you choose your lane more carefully and get through the light more quickly than the rest of the sheep around you.

In the same way, when you join a group, become a leader. Take a few extra minutes to find out the name of the group Founder/Owner. This will give you an extra edge. If the group is important enough to join, it is important enough to read the group profile and see who created it. The group owner is a leader who may know many people that you want to know. You can click on their names and look through their profiles to see if you want to connect with them.

Belonging to a group or organization that aligns with like-minded people opens many doors. My best friend Lori Hart, the Celebrity Makeup Artist, introduced me to Sara Michaels at a conference in Las Vegas. Sara, president of the Los Angeles chapter of eWomenNetwork, was having a luncheon and Founder-President Sandra Yancey was coming.

Because I was booked, I looked at Sandra's LinkedIn profile. She was named an American Hero by CNN and had international awards for making a difference than I had ever seen. She created eWomenNetwork, one of the largest and most decorated business organizations in North America, a multi-million dollar enterprise in six countries with 118 chapters helping thousands of women grow their businesses

She has won many international business and charity awards. The eWomenNetwork Foundation she created has awarded cash grants to 94 non-profit organizations and scholarships to 132 emerging female leaders. "Unlike in school," she says, "in life you don't have to come up with all the right answers. You can ask the people around you for help — or even ask them to do the things you don't do well."

I did make it to the luncheon, asked a few engaging questions and created a conversation that could be continued. I followed up with a thank you and an invite to connect on LinkedIn.

One of my favorite of her quotes is "NO is an acronym for Next Opportunity!"

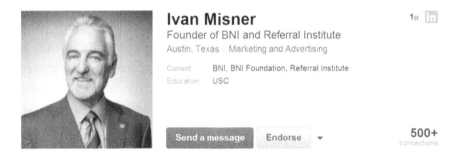

Ivan Misner 1st
Founder of BNI and Referral Institute
Austin, Texas | Marketing and Advertising

Current — BNI, BNI Foundation, Referral Institute
Education — USC

Send a message | Endorse ▼   500+ connections

Things Happen for a Reason

The day before my son passed away, he said, "Things happen for a reason." It came true for me when a friend convinced me to go to a networking meeting at the Long Beach convention center only to find it was happening the following week.

As I looked around, I saw a banner that said BNI. It's a great group, and the thought popped into my head, "Is the founder here?" Even thought it was a far-fetched coincidence, I asked the first person I saw, "By chance is Mr. Misner here?" The person said, "Yes, he is and he's standing three feet away."

To my delight I reached my hand out and said, "Hi, my name is Debra Faris It is such an honor to meet you." Now catch this. I knew BNI was a great networking group organized in 55 countries with 150,000 members to help people network, generating millions of referrals. Their LinkedIn group has over 36,000 members.

Dr. Misner is called the Father of Modern Networking. He has written 12 books, including his recent #1 bestseller, *Networking like a Pro*. He has been featured in the Wall Street Journal, the New York. Times, TV and radio shows including CNN, CNBC, and the BBC in London.

For those of you who like non-profits, he is founder of the BNI Misner Charitable Foundation and has been named Humanitarian of the Year.

Let's recap

*The **words of character** that resonate with me are:*
Commitment, Cause, Community

*What **character words** could you add about yourself?*

1. _____   2. _____   3. _____

*The **mentor/coach** I think of is Martin Luther King, Jr.*

What mentor/coach do you think of? _____

Recommended Book:
Tribes by Seth Godin

Commencements – Ellen DeGeneres
http://www.youtube.com/watch?v=0JccudODwwY

After you watched the YouTube video, what inspired you?

Your thoughts: _____

7

Follow-Up and Follow-Through

Winners make a habit of manufacturing their own positive expectations in advance of the event.

-- Brian Tracy

Brian Tracy 1st
I Help Business Owners and Entrepreneurs Achieve
Their Personal And Business Goals Faster
Greater San Diego Area   Professional Training & Coaching

Current   Brian Tracy International
Previous   5 Hour Energy
Education   University of Alberta

Send a message	Endorse ▼

500+
connections

My Influencers: Brian Tracy

"The primary reason for failure is that people do not develop new plans to replace those plans that didn't work." Napoleon Hill

In the first chapter, where I told Mike Ferry™'s story, I shared LinkedIn's awesome feature, "People also View," where members leave a trail. When I viewed Mike's profile, I noticed that people who viewed him also viewed Floyd Wickman, which led me to Tommy Hopkins, then to Brian Tracy, and then to Tony Robbins, another mentor of mine. I mention this again because it is a perfect example of a trajectory, a path that leads to successful people. It is important that you look for leaders and experts in your field, because this will be one of your gold mines or "Ahas" on LinkedIn.

Brian Tracy is a business trainer who has coached and consulted to over 1,000 companies and spoken to over 5,000,000 people in talks and seminars around the world on topics such as Entrepreneurial Success, Million Dollar Habits, Psychology of Selling, Science of Self-Confidence, Goal Setting, and Time Management. He is best-selling author of over 45 books that have been translated into dozens of languages.

At the beginning of my career, I found myself needing to learn more than I knew. First I learned the necessary skills in the education process, but I also knew I needed the other side, people skills. I need more than the "Hi, how are you?" kind of networking so many people use. I needed to learn real people skills, including the laws of success and psychology, then cross the bridge into the relationship building skills.

When I met Brian Tracy, I was learning sales during a time when most people thought of "salesman and salesperson" as bad words. They saw a "salesperson" as someone who wanted to sell them something they didn't want. The truth is we all buy things every day and, from the time we were little kids, we were selling our parents on them buying or giving us whatever we wanted. Sales psychology is part human psychology that studies why we do or want things. Sales is the art of satisfying the demand for products and services when and where they are needed.

Abraham Maslow, in "Maslow's Law," showed us that all humans have a hierarchy of basic needs. First we search for safety, then shelter, then water, then food. When we meet someone new, we follow a similar hierarchy. First we need to get to know them, then to like them, and then to trust them. As we go through this process, they get to know us, like us, and trust us. This is part of the process of "following up and following through" with everybody we meet. When we do this consistently, we create strong people skills and habits.

"Successful people are simply those with successful habits." Brian Tracy

Do you remember the movie *The Secret*? It is all about the "Law of Attraction." One of my mentors, Dr. John Demartini, who was in *The Secret*, shared with me that the law of attraction is only one of many universal laws. At that time, I used to have a university on wheels (my car) where I listen to Brian Tracy's audio program, "The Universal Laws of Success and Achievement," in which he talked about more than 100 universal laws. Using such programs to understanding the psychology of selling and to build self-confidence is a critical part of the ongoing learning process in our lives.

When you listen to audios in your car or watch late night YouTube videos late at night, you expand your awareness how communication with others helps them and helps us achieve our goals. This is a fundamental part of your personal development and your personal growth.

Why Follow-up Matters

There can be a thousand excuses why a potential contact didn't follow up with you or you didn't follow up with a new acquaintance. Either way, when follow-up doesn't happen ask yourself how your potential contact might like to be followed up with, either by phone, text, or e-mail. If you don't know, find out!

Some people may get 200 emails a day, some people have an assistant who handles their emails and that gatekeeper may have already recycled you. Don't call a person during non-business hours if you are not a personal friend because you have no personal connection. On the other hand, if you're going to meet with them at a charity run on the weekend, an after-hours call may be appropriate. If you are calling someone on a Sunday and they have Sunday reserved as a family day, you lose relationship currency.

Texting is another tricky subject. One time I was doing a favor for some people by updating their profiles on LinkedIn. When I finished, I let them know that the profile was changed and asked them to go in and check it out. I didn't hear anything from them right away so I went on with other things and figured we would catch up later. I didn't mean 3:30 a.m.! In the middle of the night, when I was fast asleep, my cell phone started squawking. OMG…who could be texting me at this horrible hour! It must be an emergency! Startled and confused, I got out of bed to check the message. What did I find? A text from one of the team members I was working with on the LinkedIn site, telling me about grammar mistakes and spelling errors. "Are you kidding me?" I thought. "It's 3:30 a.m. and they woke me up to tell me that?" I was not happy.

Remember, timing is everything. Be aware of what you're sending, when you're sending it, and how professional the content you're sending is. It can make a huge difference.

Another lesson I learned is that the bigger the person you want to contact, the more cautious and strategic you need to be in your follow-up. Asking them repeatedly for a connection or conversation will only tick them off. Once you make this mistake, you have created a negative relationship that could haunt you for years. Look at the big picture. If you are a screenwriter on a project that could take years, maybe your follow-up would be every other month. Base your follow-up timing on the players in your game of chess.

The best follow-up on LinkedIn is to send an invite. If they accept, send a thank you note and send your next step, which usually turns into a phone call opportunity. From the phone call, the next step is to meet in person. From there, take steps as the situation warrants. For instance, if you are in medical sales and you planned to meet a doctor to play a round of golf, consider the possible commission from that meeting and the possible referrals that doctor could give you to new doctors or hospitals that might use your company's products. What if that commission was worth $10,000? Ask yourself how you would approach that client. The answer is clear: Ask that client for an appointment and follow up with them. Treat them like gold. Most people miss these opportunities because they don't realize the potential of a simple first meeting. The first impression they make kills the future possibility.

14 Touch Points

In sales we have a follow up system we call the "14 touch points." In some industries, sales representatives drop off a card and a Payday candy bar. It sounds silly and simple, but consider this scenario. If it was 3 p.m. on a Friday afternoon and you loved Payday candy bars and you returned to the office to find a Payday sitting on your desk waiting for you, you would be very excited. When you notice that your sales representative delivered it because he remembered a conversation where you said you loved them, it leaves a positive feeling. You knew he was in a different city on Fridays and must have driven to your city just to drop of the candy bar before heading back to his office to turn in his required Friday reports. He just made himself your favorite rep and the next time you need to order his product, you will remember him! That 50-cent candy bar might just have made him a nice commission.

Manage your connections. What is CRM?

Once you have identified and connected with people, you then need a system to manage them. CRM is Client Retention Management. The simpler you make things, the easier they are to manage. LinkedIn has a few things that are very subtle but they are very helpful.

Here are my top three:

1. When you connect with someone or they connect with you, in the invitations list it will show they accepted. I use this as a way to keep track of my invitations.

2. When you look at the list of your connections, LinkedIn shows them by various categories. You can sort by recent

conversation, last name, first name or new. You can also find by tags, all in lower case, such as friends, groups, members, colleagues, partners, classmates, and untagged. LinkedIn created this default because your connections connected with you through one of these categories or you connected with them through one of these categories.

Tags

★ Emanuel Gonzales ★ 1st
Founder-Speaker-Coach at Emanuel Gonzales International
Greater Los Angeles Area

🏷 mt @ james malinchak   🏷 my linkedin attendee's

Michelle Patterson 1st
President at California Women's Conference
Orange County, California Area

🏷 speaker   🏷 top 100   🏷 website

Bob Watson | CRB | @TopBrokerOC 1st
Founder & Facilitator at Social Media Mastermind Orange County-SMMOC & SMMOC-RE
Orange County, California Area

🏷 ask 4 recommendations   🏷 my linkedin attendee's   🏷 real estate   🏷 smmoc   🏷 top 100

JIM |(MBA-GRI) ....Orange Co.,Ca. 1st
District Mgt for Real Estate Services and Hort. at Carter-Hawley-Hale |
Orange County, California Area

🏷 new oc 1

3. Tags: The way you use them will evolve as your networking grows. Here are a few ways you can tag people:
    a) Top companies: tag the people that you are connected to so you can come back another time
    b) People with phone numbers
    c) People that share a group you can network with
    d) Key people that live or work in the city or community

e) People you met that you need to follow up with
f) Recruiters
g) Alumni

Ask, Ask, Ask for Help and Referrals

The biggest challenge that is I see people have when they network is also one of the three biggest challenges people have in communication. This is true for everyone, male or female, young or old. They have great difficulty saying:

1. I love you
2. I'm sorry
3. Can you help me?

We seem to forget our purpose when we are networking. For example, if you are looking for a job, after you have identified your contact and built a relationship, you must be clear when you request help and ask specifically what you are looking for. The key is to ask! If you want the person to introduce you to the Dean at the Law School you are thinking of attending….ask! If you want to connect through LinkedIn to a CEO at a company you want to work for after you graduate, ask for an introduction. Use your connections to your benefit. "Can you connect me with John Smith? He's the Vice President of Merchandising and I'm thinking about applying there in six months." Send two simple sentences to someone in your network who knows John Smith and who knows, you might just get an interview.

Who are your Top Five Companies?

In networking, part of your pitch is to share what company you would like to work for. Even more important than your pitch is your follow-up. Make a list of five to seven different ways you can share your mission with people. Ask yourself why

Be larger than your task.
Orison Sweet Marden

you want to work for them. Re-read the job description and find out what they are looking for. Tailor your follow up specifically to what they want.

Example:

Dear Mr. Brown,

I am in my 2nd year at USC and enjoying the experience. Although I know it will be two years before I graduate I have started to identify jobs and companies that interest me now and I have begun to prepare myself. In my search, I found this marketing job and I would like to prepare myself to be a top candidate on your list when I graduate. I want to thank you in advance for the opportunity and ask that if you know of anyone or any LinkedIn group that can help me on my path, please share my information with them and help me on my mission.

Thank you again for accepting my LinkedIn invite.
I hope to be an added contributor to many others in the future.
Signed by you
(Your current email address)
(Your current phone number)

It was character that got us out of bed, commitment that moved us into action, and discipline that enabled us to follow through.

Zig Ziglar

Identify the top five companies you want to work for after college. Research them and identify jobs within these organizations that interest you. Find the names of people in these organizations and see if they are on LinkedIn. If so, see if anyone you're connected to is connected to them. Search the actual companies on LinkedIn and see if they have a LinkedIn presence or have available jobs listed. Many companies use LinkedIn to list job opportunities. Find out everything you can about the five companies you have identified and become a top candidate for them as you finish school.

Make a list of your top 20 connections

Have you ever met a person and later said to yourself, "I wish I had followed up or I should have stayed in touch with…" When I was in my 20s, a real estate broker said to me, "If you have 100 people who like you, know you and trust you, you won't be looking for a job or a friend."

Companies

USA TODAY
Newspapers
✓ Following

American Marketing …
Marketing and Advertising
✓ Following

Umpqua Bank
Banking
✓ Following

Verizon
Information Technology and Services
✓ Following

Ocean Bank
Banking
✓ Following

AV Event Solutions
Events Services
✓ Following

Peak Potentials
Professional Training & Coaching
✓ Following

National College Plan…
Education Management
✓ Following

Sears Home Services
Consumer Services
✓ Following

Boston Private Bank
Banking
✓ Following

Udemy
E-Learning
✓ Following

Chevron
Oil & Energy
✓ Following

Dell
Information Technology and Services
✓ Following

Socal BNI
Professional Training & Coaching
✓ Following

Dale Carnegie Training
Professional Training & Coaching
✓ Following

HDFC Bank
Banking
✓ Following

As life passes, we see many changes along our path. Friends move, we move, we lose touch. One of my challenges was that after

30 years I hadn't keep in touch with many of my early contacts. I had missed many opportunities. There's a saying I like a lot: "You can save a lot of time (time is money) if you learn from someone else's mistake." LinkedIn makes it easy to stay in touch with people, even those you lost contact with long ago. In the section on connecting, I showed you a memory jogger that helps you rediscover people you met in your past and recent present. Begin by making a list of people you have connected with at your various jobs. The memory jogger will also help when you do your CRM (Client Retention Management). You can use this as you develop your 100 top people. Since you are new at developing your relationships, this list will shift based on how future relationships and alignments develop as you meet more people.

Here is the recipe for who could be good resources for job connections:

- Four recruiters
- Four alumni
- Four current employees
- Four people from groups

President Reagan wrote Five Thank You notes a day

Ronald Reagan was the 40th President of the United States and was one of our oldest presidents. Prior to his presidency, he served as the 33rd Governor of California. When he ran for office a common comment was, "Is this a joke?" because he had been on radio, television and in movies. Could a celebrity really run the country?

I believe that you can get everything in life you want if you will just help enough other people get what they want.

Zig Ziglar

Not only was President Reagan one of our favorite presidents, he also had a gift for connecting with people.

His style was to make connections personal so that people never forgot him. One of his professional business habits was to write five thank-you notes every day.

On LinkedIn, writing a thank-you is a wonderful way to start your relationships with new connections. When you say "thank you" and acknowledge your new LinkedIn friend or future colleagues, you are well on your way to building a personal relationship with them.

Craft scripts & Templates

Invite **Jill** to connect on LinkedIn

How do you know Jill?

○ Colleague
○ Classmate
○ We've done business together
○ Friend
● Groups
   Social Media Marketing

○ Other
○ I don't know Jill

Include a personal note: (optional)

Jill
We not only share a group together, but are alumni of the same college) I see that you are no longer in California, will you be coming to California in the next few months? Perhaps we can grab a cup of coffee?

- Debra Faris

Invitation with a Personal Note

Let's recap

*The **words of character** that resonate with me are:*
Consistency, Discipline, Determination

*What **character words** could you add about yourself?*

1._____ 2. _____ 3. _____

*The **mentor/coach** I think of is Helen Keller.*

What mentor/coach do you think of? _____

Recommended Book:
Endless Referrals by Bob Burg

Commencements – Arianna Huffington
http://www.youtube.com/watch?v=UJ25qEHgcM4

After you watched the YouTube video, what inspired you?

Your thoughts: _____

8

Recommendations, Marketing

Marketing is not an event, but a process... It has a beginning, a middle, but never an end, for it is a process. You improve it, perfect it, change it, even pause it. But you never stop it completely.

--J. Conrad Levinson

 **David T. Fagan**   2nd

Icon Builder Media ♦ International Speaker ♦ Guerrilla Marketing ♦ Digital Magazine ♦ Brand Development ♦ Celebrity PR ♦

Beverly Hills, California   Professional Training & Coaching

Current	Icon Builder Media
Previous	Levine Communications Office, Cutting Edge Ventures LLC (Trilogy), Guerrilla Marketing
Education	University of Phoenix

Connect   Send David T. InMail   ▾   **500+**
                                                            connections

My Influencers: David Fagan

It's not what you know, but who you know. Or better yet... who knows you! I've been so blessed, in so many ways, mostly from having great coaches and mentors along the way.

Jim Rohn says, "You are the sum total of your closest friends." One of my friends and coach is Bob Donnell, who presented a business builder event where I had the honor of being one of the three experts. Another of the experts was David Fagan, a family man with eight kids, all with his wife Jill. I know he attributes his success to his kids. He is always sharing things like, "Kids teach you as much as you teach them" and "my kids keep me humble and grateful."

David is the author of *Cracking the ICON CODE*, where he shares the story of how he was a major contributor to and CEO of the largest, most successful series of marketing books, *Guerrilla Marketing* by Jay Conrad Levinson. Jay was one of the first real marketing gurus, known for branding the Marlboro Man, Charlie the Tuna, and Tony the Tiger among others.

David went on to work with and purchase Michael Levine's 30-year-Hollywood public relations agency, which has represented 58 Academy Award winners, 34 Grammy winners and 42 New York Times best sellers, and a client list that ranges from Bill Clinton, Michael Jackson, Dave Chappelle, *Playboy*, Sean "P Diddy" Combs and brands like Nike. David teaches in his book and at his events that you must use your brain and brand, know your market and

> *If your imagination leads you to understand how quickly people grant your requests when those requests appeal to their self-interest, you can have practically anything you go after.*
> **Napoleon Hill**

your fans, and most importantly use the "Law of Multiplication."

When I asked David what secret he most wanted to share with college students as they stepped into their new future, he said, "It is always easier to help someone else than yourself. Get involved with a power group or someone outside your circle that can give you good feedback."

David also said what energized him through his journey was to celebrate his little wins by going to dinner. When one of his kids got a win, they got to pick a favorite movie.

"We all celebrated together," he says. "But what's most important is that you have to celebrate along the way."

Market like an Icon

Nike. Speedo. Coke. McDonald's. Nordstrom. Guess.

What do all of these names have in common? They're brands we recognize without any explanation. We know what they are, what they represent, and how to use them. Developing your profile on LinkedIn is a form of branding. You're telling people who you are, what you represent, and how to use you in the future. Getting your brand across correctly is an important step. Finding the right words to communicate the right message is critical to your success.

Here's an example of branding from the banking business. Let's say someone has been successful in the home loan business. Now she wants to become a business developer so she introduces herself this way, "Hi! My name is Nancy, I used to work for Bank of America doing home loans, but what I really want to do is to work with Chase as a business developer."

What is the one thing that people will remember about her? That she is in home loans. Don't tell people what you don't want them to remember. Craft your statement very carefully to remove what you don't want and emphasize what you do want, in this case a position with Chase.

In your LinkedIn profile, tie the job description you want to everything in your profile. You may ask, "How do I make my future self into who I am now?"

It's not that hard, but it takes some thinking. You must ask the right questions to get the right answers. You tell people that you are seeking a position in whatever it is you want to do even though a lot of people say that you shouldn't do that. If you are looking for a position, you need to talk to people who know where the open positions are. You need to work on how you present your need. You may say that you "aspire for a position in...." which doesn't say you are a job seeker.

Furthermore, you need to remember that what you have done in the past has brought you to where you are today. List the places where you have volunteered, the places you have interned, and the places you have worked for. Be sure to include what you desire in all of your explanations. Tie your past into your future. This will brand you for what you want to become so people will think of you when they see the open position you are seeking.

Credibility through Celebrity

> *What the mind of man can conceive and believe, the mind of man can achieve.*
> **Napoleon Hill**

Reality television shows are popular because they show how ordinary people can establish credibility through celebrity. It is a silent recommendation. If you are connected with celebrities, you must be a celebrity yourself. This is why you see so many celebrity product endorsements. It's tribal communication, meaning no words are exchanged. If a person you respect and admire likes a product or person, that product or person must be good. Why else would the celebrity endorse it?

The key point for college students is that when you associate in any way with celebrities, you become more attractive to your peers and to potential employers. At first you may know only local celebrities, like the college chancellor or the student body president. They may lead you to other even more influential celebrities like business leaders, who can ease your way into the job market. Here are three examples of how persons who started out as non-celebrities used connections with celebrities become more credible and even become celebrities themselves. It's a great demonstration of credibility through celebrity.

Twenty years ago, I met Jay Bennett, a home business coach and mentor and a trainer for multi-level marketers, through a network marketing company, Quorum, which was owned by Raymond Hung, one of the wealthiest entrepreneurs in Hong Kong. Jay worked in many Multi-Level Marketing companies, starting with Herbalife. Network Marketing companies have always attracted personal development and leadership people; and it's always been part of their coaching and training to get new distributors.

Jay taught me that it is easier to promote someone else than to promote yourself; just like it's easier to take photos of your friends than to shoot "selfies." If you have not yet made a million dollars, it makes no sense to promote yourself as a coach who can create millionaires. However, if you associate yourself with millionaires by getting yourself photographed with them, taking courses from them, or getting into masterminds with them, people will listen to you.

Even as a college student, you have opportunities to meet and associate with millionaires, such as visiting celebrities on campus, large donors to the college, and social events where they may appear to show support for education. Celebrities tend to become role models for society. People accept what they see from celebrities, in many cases without verifying whether the information they hear is true or not. Having a celebrity brag about you and tell others how great you are will make your job search easier. If one of the people in your network is a celebrity and they decide to promote you, think of how much that helps you in your quest!

I shared in the chapter on networking a new connection who is not only my mentor but my friend. Another way to meet celebrities is through your friends who may be connected with celebrities. I've been to several dinner parties this new connection has hosted and met several celebrities there.

One of my favorite celebrities from those dinner parties is Glenn Morshower, best known for playing Secret Service Agent Aaron Pierce in 24. He has also been in *The Transformers* and *Grizzly Park*, always playing the colonel or the tough guy. It is fascinating to me that actors can shift easily into film roles even though in reality they are nothing like the characters they play. Glenn is the farthest thing from being a tough guy. He is a very funny man, with a memory like a fox.

He started out like everyone else, completely unknown. In his early days at auditions, he would go out for parts and not get them. He would study and work, but success eluded him. Then one day he put syrup in his shoes and he got the part. "Hmm," he thought, "Let's try something else." Next he put cornflakes in his shoes and got the part. His wife was always part of his scheme and helped fill his shoes to insure he would get the part. Since his schemes were working, every time he auditioned he would create a ridiculous scheme to anchor himself. These games gave him the self-confidence he needed to start getting parts and build his own celebrity.

One of today's most recognized seminar speakers is James Malinchak, famous for being on the *Secret Millionaire* television show. He trademarks himself as a Big Money speaker, and has created his *Big Money Speaker Boot Camp*, and his *College Speaker Success Boot Camp*. In both events, he develops and trains entrepreneurs to speak, coach, and build or improve their businesses. James is known for his philanthropic charitable gifts. In the *Secret Millionaire*, James helped three families get back on their feet with generous donations.

> *Luck is what happens when preparation meets opportunity.*
> **Seneca**

However, James was not always a celebrity. I remember him years ago speaking on small seminar stages to build his reputation. Unlike most of these speakers, James knew that to build celebrity, he needed to associate with celebrities. In the beginning, such opportunities were rare but he took advantage of every one. It only takes a single connection to open the door and for James one connection led to many more.

Now he brings many celebrities he has met over the years to his events to share their message with the speakers and entrepreneurs in the audience.

One of my favorite celebrity speakers is Les Brown, whose events I've attended for over 20 years. He is often a guest speaker at Malinchak's events and the crowds love him. On the sports side, I enjoy hearing James' good friend Joe Theismann, a former National Football League quarterback. Theismann is the subject of several highly popular sports videos on YouTube showing the tragic, career-ending football injury he suffered in 1985. He teaches audiences that even after game changing events, you can turn your life into a huge success. James connects celebrities with his audiences and teaches them how to gain credibility by increasing their own celebrity connections. By using his celebrity connections, James Malinchak also gives his own event credibility.

You as a college student can give yourself credibility by finding and connecting with celebrities in the field you want to enter. They are not hard to find or meet if you position yourself correctly.

People Also Viewed

When you were a little kid did anyone ever tell you a fish story? My dad actually told me once we were going on a snipe hunt. We had to wait until the sun went down and it was dark. We had to be quiet and were searching for snipes with a flashlight. We put our shoes on grabbed our flashlights and pillow cases and headed out into the night to catch our snipes.

Lo and behold, my father had me outside calling for snipe but all I heard was a cricket. After 30 minutes my dad said there must not be any snipes out tonight and we came in. Later that summer he took me fishing. He gave me a fishing pole, taught me how to bait the hook and propped me up on a quaint little bridge. Then he tromped off in his golf shoes to shoot nine holes of golf. When he

People Also Viewed

Katishia Cosley Trigg
Show Host at KTRK, Live Well Network

Ellie Scarborough Brett
founder at Media Bombshell

Lauren Freeman
Anchor at KPRC-TV

Kym Forester
Membership Director at National Insurance Crime Bureau

Anjuli Lohn
Reporter at FOX 13 WTVT-TV

Katie McCall
Reporter & Fill-in Anchor at Fox 26 Houston

Deborah Bussell
Business Development Manager at The Next Up

Annie Velasquez
Otter Relations Business Partner at OtterBox

Sarah Cole
Licensed Realtor at Harcourts Prime Properties

Dominique Sachse
News Anchor at KPRC-TV

returned, I told him I had caught three fish. He shook his head. What happened was I did catch one fish but when I pulled him up and he hit the ground, a small fish popped out of this first fish and an even smaller fish came out.

Shared stories are bridge builders. This is one of my top 20 favorite functions on LinkedIn. On LinkedIn, when you as a viewer look at a person's profile, it shows you other people that that this person's viewers also viewed. For example, if you look up Oprah Winfrey, it may show you other talk show hosts that people also viewed. My favorite story of "Who knows Who" goes back to when I received an invite from the most successful real estate coach in the United States, CEO and real estate coach Mike Ferry™. When I looked at his profile, I noticed that people also viewed Floyd Wickman and when I clicked on Floyd I saw that people viewed Tommy Hopkins and when I viewed Tommy I saw people viewed Brian Tracy and when I clicked on Brian I saw that people viewed Tony Robbins and that put the biggest smile on my face because Tony was one of my mentors. :) When you use the "People Also Viewed" feature on LinkedIn, you identify people that you may not know but may need in your job search. Look at the "People Also Viewed" feature when doing research on LinkedIn and you may find some valuable connections.

> *For every force, there is a counter force, for every negative there is a positive, for every action there is a reaction. For every cause there is an effect.*
> **Grace Speare**

Who knows Who

While viewing the profiles of potential recruiters, you may see something you like, maybe one of their second-level connections or someone who gave them a recommendation, someone they recommended, or maybe someone who endorsed them. You realize that you too want to connect with that person. When you click on that person's name or picture to look at their profile, it creates a path for spiders, the bits of software that track all LinkedIn activity. At the end of the day those paths are added up and you become part of the list of people who most viewed that person's profile. This is important because it is part of the social proof that begins with ripples, becomes rivers, and leads to tribes in this arena of online presence. Most of us are curious about who likes whom or who follows whom because in the job-searching world, that person may be the one who is one or two degrees or levels away from introducing us to our dream job. This applies to any activity, including hobbies, romance, and recreation.

Keep in Touch Marketing

In the Real Estate industry, a common practice is to send out a monthly newsletter. In other industries, companies send holiday postcards on special occasions every month, including Valentine's Day, Easter, St. Patrick's Day, Christmas, and Thanksgiving. All these cards include a special message advertising the company's service or specials.

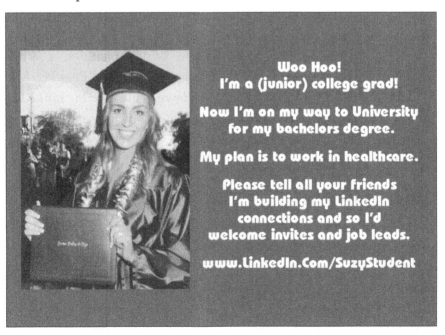

Woo Hoo!
I'm a (junior) college grad!

Now I'm on my way to University
for my bachelors degree.

My plan is to work in healthcare.

Please tell all your friends
I'm building my LinkedIn
connections and so I'd
welcome invites and job leads.

www.LinkedIn.Com/SuzyStudent

Even the owner of a small business starting out on a shoestring budget from his kitchen table can do this. This business owner will use Vistaprint to get his first set of business cards at a reasonable price. The next step for him is to print advertising postcards with photos of dogs wearing silly hats, cats dressed up in costumes, and even bearded dragons wearing dresses. Why? So he can make his business memorable.

This works on LinkedIn as well. Wouldn't it be cool if you updated your friends and family at the Holidays with not just a photo of your newest outfit but a real update? Maybe you aced your hardest test. Maybe you put lights and reindeer ears on your car. Share your events with "Photo

Marketing" cards. Then, six months later, you can do even more updates. Send your friends and family your "School's out for summer" update and fall update: "I'm a Junior! Moving on to Grad School! No More tests!!" If you know the companies you're interested in working with you can send the contacts from those companies your LinkedIn Profile.

Recommendations

Received (23) ▾   Given (3)

Networking & LinkedIn Coach
The Chief Networking Officer

Andrea L. Russo
I am your ambassador of first impressions actively seeking a career position working with Seniors in my local area

❝ Debra recently spoke at my church where I was a former "Hospitality Coordinator" there with Career Renewal Ministries. She was truly amazing! She shared personal stories that were so empowering and motivating. Her knowledge and expertise with navigating through the proper usage and getting the most out of your Linkedin page proved to be invaluable to me. Thank you again... **more**

January 16, 2014, Andrea L. worked directly with Debra at The Chief Networking Officer

★Batista Gremaud★
Body Design Formula Leadership Team Builder and Visionary ♦ Author ♦

❝ Debra Farris is most qualified and knowledgeable in the Linkedin applications. She has helped me personally create an appealing profile and has shared with me some very valuable strategies. I recommend her to anyone who wants to use Linkedin to accelerate their business growth and amplify their social media presence.
Batista Gremaud
Body Design Formula - Dr Fitness USA

January 31, 2013, ★Batista was with another company when working with Debra at The Chief Networking Officer

Patti Langell
Contributor at Hollywood52.com | Social Media Consultant | Social Entrepreneur

❝ I have taken many courses on using Linkedin and I felt confident that I was more knowledgeable than most on the best practices for using it. Then I met Debra Faris and took a Linkedin course from her. All I can say is wow! She showed me things I know most Linkedin trainers don't even know how to do. It takes a lot to impress me since I have been around social media for a... **more**

January 9, 2013, Patti was Debra's client

Who did they recommend & who recommended them?

In the banking and loan business, a lender will ask for two years of tax returns or six months of previous utility bills to verify that payments were made in the manner necessary to grant the credit on a loan.

In the world of LinkedIn, when it comes to verifying a person's depth of experience, nothing speaks louder than recommendations from former colleagues and bosses. Using your network to build up strong recommendations is an important piece of the LinkedIn puzzle. When a potential employer sees a recommendation on your profile, it gives your resume extra validation and verification.

On the other hand, who have you recommended? Are you giving endorsements to the right individuals for the right reasons? When employers see who you have endorsed and recommended, they may also use this information in their decision-making process.

Testimonials are your best friend

The biggest question I get concerns my opinion on swapping recommendations. I admit that at first I didn't like the idea but when I thought about it, it seemed logical in certain situations.

Let's say I invested a lot of time coaching a client and gave them a tip that made them a very substantial amount of money and then realized that they had mentored me years before through a book they wrote that a helped hundreds, thousands, or millions of people, including myself. I would want a recommendation from that person for the work I did and would not hesitate to give them one knowing the value of the services he had performed for me.

My answer to that question is simple. Was value exchanged? I won't write a general recommendation for you nor expect one from you if nothing of value happened. I would only recommend you if I personally experienced your value and can in good conscience stand behind the recommendation. Back in Chapter 1, "Who Am I," I showed you that if you were a Boy or Girl Scout and your scoutmaster had known you for years and knew your character well, they would

Thoughts and Tips

Keep a separate notebook.
Track people who you want to meet.

Check off each one to whom you sent a connection.
Check off every sent message to one of them.

Join a group that you like and they like.
Follow some of their companies.

definitely stand behind their recommendation. The best recommendations come from people with the integrity to give an unequivocal positive recommendation.

Be a producer using iPhone Videos

Have you ever used your cell phone to look up a YouTube video and then shared it with your friends because it meant something or was funny? By encouraging users to post videos and photos on the site, LinkedIn has made it easier for us to use technology to bring us to life for the world to see just like people on the big screen and on reality television. Make your profile more eye-catching by adding video. People love to watch movies, television, and YouTube. Let them watch a video of you!

Although the Baby Boomers are still trying to catch up to Generation Y in technology, LinkedIn has made it easier. Since we use our cell phones for everything now, including pictures and videos, we can make high quality visual presentations that make us all look professional on LinkedIn.

Let's recap

*The **words of character** that resonate with me are:*
<u>Trustworthy</u>, <u>Value</u>, <u>Service</u>

*What **character words** could you add about yourself?*

1._____ 2. _____ 3. _____

*The **mentor/coach** I think of is <u>Dale Carnegie.</u>*

What mentor/coach do you think of? _____

Recommended Book:
Eat That Frog by Brian Tracy

Commencements – Sanjay Gupta
*http://www.youtube.com/watch?v=QJxmLSjoPYg&list=PL54F0
8A8E49DBC917*

After you watched the YouTube video, what inspired you?

Your thoughts: _____

9

The Power of
Charity and Volunteering

Let us not be satisfied with just giving money. Money is not enough,
money can be got, but they need your hearts to love them. So, spread
your love everywhere you go.
-- Mother Teresa

▶ **Jim Palmer** ◀   1st

★ Committed to Helping One Million Homeless ★ CEO
Orange County Rescue Mission a Non-Profit Organization

Orange County, California Area | Nonprofit Organization Management

Current	Hurtt Family Health Clinics a Non-Profit Organization, County of Orange Housing Authority & Community Resources, Orange County Rescue Mission
Previous	OC Partnership to End Homelessness, Corporation for National and Community Service, City of Tustin
Education	Corona del Mar High School

[Send a message ▼]   500+
                                                     connections

My Influencers: Jim Palmer

Have you ever tried to be neighborly but found that one of your neighbors seemed less than welcoming? You might have asked

106

yourself, "What's wrong with them?" When this happens we need to resist the urge to make snap assumptions. Sometimes we don't know how or why sparrows have broken wings.

One of my favorite people in the charity world is Jim Palmer. Very few people in this world understood their mission as early as Jim Palmer. At the age of 14 years old, Jim found out that his next door neighbor could not make their house payment and were going to lose their home. The father had died, leaving the family with no income. His heart bled for the children, who he thought would become homeless, and wondered where they would sleep, how they would find food, and who would protect them. That started him on his mission to help the homeless.

Charity means love. "The least, the last, and the lost." Jim Palmer's organization helps them all. Jim is the CEO of Orange County Rescue Mission, a Christian Haven helping people in Orange County get off the streets forever. When people hit bottom, they face the most difficult time of their lives. They've lost their job, their home and have nowhere

Karma is the eternal assertion of human freedom...Our thoughts, our words, and deeds are the threads of the net which we throw around ourselves.
Swami Vivekananda

to go. Orange County Rescue Mission helps them. When people show up addicted to drugs or alcohol, Orange County Rescue Mission helps them find rehab centers and takes them back after they've followed the programs. When people who had addictions and worked their way through rehab are ready to rejoin the community, Orange County Rescue Mission helps.

Each year the Mission saves over 200 lives. People know they can count on breakfast, lunch, and dinner for their children and a roof over their heads. I went to a recent graduation and listened and learned how people who had no hope, no family, even single moms with babies, were able to start over in their communities and build life skills that will help them be more productive. The OCRM puts those who have a child to work in their daycare program. Others are given jobs inside the program with no phone privileges, specific bed times, and time windows for meals to get them back on track and put the idea of keeping a schedule back into their lives. Some of OCRM's clients graduate from two-year colleges or trade schools with skills that get them jobs as their lives go forward. These people in turn help others and create the ripple effect that saves lives.

When you make a paradigm shift to adopt the mindset that you are here to make a difference, to help the other people, your entire LinkedIn visibility will change. When you use the fundamentals I have given you in this book, your LinkedIn profile will stand out like you paid $1,000 dollars to a professional to create it. The important part of LinkedIn is its ability to help you build relationships.

In this chapter, I will teach you to build relationships and build a profile that will make a difference to others. If you help somebody today, they will remember you in the future. Think back to what you did last summer. Was it just a break from the rigors of class work? Yes, I know summer is the time to take a break. However, you don't have to give away your whole summer. Just plan two or three projects like a clean- the-beach day or national-pet-adoption week or go to a boys or girls club to help them enjoy a safe Fourth of July. It doesn't take much, but what you do will resonate with those you helped forever.

Attitude of Gratitude

Last year, as I was preparing to send out my annual Thanksgiving letters, I found an old letter in which I wrote about giving thanks to my friends and remembering a time when I had nothing.

One of my girlfriends went to Hawaii for three months and let me live in her condo in Santa Monica. At the time I had no job and no income. The condo was free but I was still responsible for the electricity, the gas, and the utilities.

Later, as Thanksgiving approached, I called a few of my friends to catch up. I told one of my friends that I wasn't sure what I was going to do about Thanksgiving because my oven didn't work. She told me not to worry, that she had it under control. She brought over a roasting pan (the kind that that you plug in) and a turkey and we roasted the turkey. As I reconnected with my friends in the weeks prior to Thanksgiving, everybody worked together and on the big day, all of them brought food. We created a feast fit for a king! We played games, laughed, and joked. It was the best Thanksgiving ever! It started out as a Thanksgiving where I had nothing and became an incredibly memorable day with friends and food. What more could I have asked for? I was so thankful.

When you approach life with an "attitude of gratitude" you will be surprised at how much you really do have. Changing the way you look at life will drive you to be more successful than you ever imagined. Many times we look at our lives and are unhappy because we're focused on the wrong parts. Focus on the positive, have an attitude of gratitude, and be thankful for what you have.

Tony Robbins, one of my mentors, has a similar mission statement on his Tony Robbins International Basket Brigade website. It is one of the ways Tony Robbins *chooses* to make a difference: "The International Basket Brigade is built on a simple notion: one small act of generosity on the part of one caring person can transform the lives of hundreds." What began as Tony's individual effort to feed families in need has now grown to the point where his campaign provides baskets of food and household items for an estimated two million people annually in countries all over the world.

I'm reminded of my friend, motivational speaker and author Michael J. Herman, who shared a story with me about one Christmas Eve when he and his wife Penny filled up their car with food and from the back of their car fed 68 homeless and hungry people living on Skid Row. Out of that experience of altruism and while creating a project to benefit the community through

Landmark Education's Self Expression and Leadership Course, Herman's program, The Needy Smorgasbord Project, was born.

The next Christmas Eve, Herman and his wife brought an army of more than 100 friends and volunteers along with donations from almost 50 restaurants and stores to feed homeless, hungry, and needy people. Now this nationwide movement reaches tens of thousands in need. The outcomes were possible because Herman sought to help others. This story of generosity touched me so much that I invited Michael to partner with me on a book about giving and philanthropy.

Can you see how little movements like these can change the world? Can you see how you have within you the greatness and the power to build structures and systems for change and abundance?

Yes, you do!

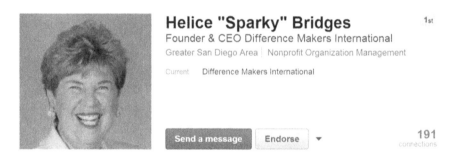

Helice "Sparky" Bridges   1st
Founder & CEO Difference Makers International
Greater San Diego Area | Nonprofit Organization Management

Current   Difference Makers International

Send a message   Endorse   ▼   **191**
                                            connections

You Have a Calling

Like random acts of kindness, being at the right place at the right time is critical. My mentor coach Bob Donnell invited me to his inner circle where I met a personality as big as her nickname, Sparky. She gave me a huge heart hug.

"In 1979," she told me, "I was married, had two pre-teen sons, a successful career and a beautiful home overlooking the Pacific Ocean. But no matter how much money I made, I had to live with a husband who controlled, intimidated and verbally abusive me. I was spiritually and emotionally broken. I had no way out. On the very day I decided to commit suicide, I heard a voice inside me say,

"You cannot take your life because you are going to make a big difference in the world."

That changed her life. After she divorced her husband, she founded Difference Makers International and created a way to show people how to express appreciation, respect and love for themselves and others which has impacted over 40 million people throughout the world, eradicating bullying, preventing adolescent suicide and helping make dreams come true. She has just launched a global project – One Billion Dreams Coming True by 2020.

What's your Cause?

Since one of my mentors has always been Mother Teresa, I have a huge compassion for the homeless.

I don't if anybody knows the actual percentage of homeless people who are mentally ill. Still, it breaks my heart that they don't know how to properly take care of or fend for themselves. When we care for each other, it's hard for us to see someone else suffering and in need and not take some kind of action.

> *Compassion will cure more sins than condemnation.*
> **Henry Ward Beecher**

One time I was driving by McDonald's and realized my dog needed water so I ran in quickly to get him some water. Before I could open the door to the restaurant, I saw a homeless woman with different color socks, wearing a poncho, unkempt hair, with a shopping cart filled with her treasures, items others would see as junk. I instantly stopped and asked her if she was hungry. We caught each other's eyes and she said yes. I thought that buying this woman a meal would be an easy task for me. However, I realized I hadn't gone to the bank and I was standing there with no cash and no debit card.

I decided to use my resourcefulness and ask the cashier if she might have something she could give to this homeless person. She said no. I explained to the cashier that I had no money on me but this woman was hungry and homeless. She said no again. I asked to see the manager.

The manager came out from behind the counter and in an abrupt manner said, "What do you want?"

I said to him, "There's a homeless woman here who's hungry. You must have something here that can help her. You must have something in the warmer that isn't on order."

He again said no.

"Do you understand that this is a human being who lives in your community? I find it hard to believe you would let someone go hungry."

 Volunteer Experience & Causes

Co-Chair
Afghan Amity Society fundraiser
January 2010 – August 2012 (2 years 8 months) | Children

Co-Chair Laguna Beach for Afghan Amity Society fundraiser. Arranged for 20 artists for event with speaker, world renowned humanist Dr. Masaru Emaoto. Afghan Amity has now helped over 600 women and children in Herat, Afghanistan, to get an education and clean, healthy water to villages in Afghanistan. Can you imagine... If we could get clean water to all that need, we would save 2 million lives a year.

Opportunities you are looking for:

• Joining a nonprofit board

Causes you care about:

• Animal Welfare
• Children
• Economic Empowerment
• Education
• Human Rights
• Women protection against Domestic Violence
• Protecting Wild Life
• Arts & Music for Children
• Homeless with Mental Illness
• Creating Leaders for the Next Generation

Organizations you support:

• Orange County Rescue Mission
• Best Friends Animal Society
• Disabled American Veterans
• Helping Children Worldwide
• Special Olympics
• NAMI
• A Mission For Michael

He said, "It's our policy."

At this point I found myself so frustrated with McDonald's that I started to ask the patrons in the store if they wanted to contribute to buy her lunch. While the woman stood next to me with a sad expression on her face, I asked four tables for help and could not get one person to say yes. I looked at a man who had three cheeseburgers on his tray and asked if he wanted to give her one. He said no.

At this point I was beginning to feel like a failure. All I wanted to do was feed someone who had no food and I couldn't even help this one poor woman. My frantic

> *I have found that among its other benefits, giving liberates the soul of the giver.*
> **Maya Angelou**

energy must have been bouncing off the walls. In the distance, I saw an Asian couple and heard them speaking to each other but I couldn't understand them. For whatever reason, I hadn't bothered to ask them for help knowing it might be difficult for them to understand me.

However, they did understand my desperate desire. The woman stood and walked over to me and said, "...food...she food...she food?" She pointed at the food and then at the homeless lady.

I said, "Yes, yes," nodding my head up and down.

She said, "I I I," and tapped her chest. All I could say was thank you.

As I watched, the lady told the man, "Meal meal meal," then walked to the counter and bought the homeless lady a meal.

The lady looked at the Asian woman and said, "God bless you."

What's your cause? Helping the homeless, working with underprivileged children, and working with animals that have been rescued are just a few of the causes supported by thousands of charity organizations you can get involved with. Decide what pulls at your heart strings the most and then commit to helping others.

Random Act of Kindness

One of my favorite things to do is always carry a protein bar in my glove box. It's simple and easy and it doesn't matter where I am. If I pull into a shopping center and see a homeless person sitting there, I say, "Hey, I have one of these great protein bars. Do you want one?" They almost always say yes.

> *Since you get more joy out of giving joy to others, you should put a good deal of thought into the happiness that you are able to give.*
> **Eleanor Roosevelt**

One day I was eating at a pancake house with my daughter and our breakfast cost $15, which left me with $10. We figured our meal was cheap but her service was extremely top notch so we left her the $10 and said, "Thanks! You made our morning delightful." She smiled and said, "You made mine off to a great start."

When we walked out the door we saw a homeless man lying on the grass. He had no socks and his shoes were so worn they looked like they were going to fall off his feet. His hair and beard were both matted and dirty, but through his tattered and torn clothes you could tell they were hanging loose on his body, an indication of malnutrition. It broke my heart, but I had given the waitress the last of my money. I looked around to see if there was another way I could get help for him.

Five different sets of people were standing outside the restaurant waiting for their name to get called to eat their breakfast. I went from family to family asking, "Do you see that homeless man over there? Would you be willing to give him a couple bucks so he could get something to eat?" One by one they all either said no or turned away, I got so frustrated that people who were going to fill their bellies would allow someone to go hungry right in front of them.

Finally the door opened and out walked a very young couple, probably college students. They looked like they were in love or certainly were having a very nice time. I felt silly asking them because it was probably a treat for them to spend the money to go out to breakfast.

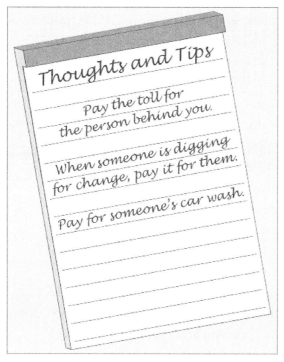

Thoughts and Tips

Pay the toll for the person behind you.

When someone is digging for change, pay it for them.

Pay for someone's car wash.

I asked anyway. The young man said, "We just used our debit card."

I got it, but then I noticed that they had taken their leftovers. I said, "I know this sounds weird, but do you really think you'll eat those leftovers? I know half the time I think I will eat them but half the time I don't. Why don't you go over there and ask him if he wants them?"

I had done what I could and walked back to my car. As I got to my car I looked back and saw the homeless guy already eating the food. I smiled ear to ear. I turned the car on, pulled out of the parking lot, and drove down the street. Just as I was about to make a U-turn I heard a honk-honk-honk. It was the young couple, my giving sweet new human connections, waving to me. I could feel their smile and their happiness that they knew they had made a difference.

Later my daughter said, "You know how to bring the best out in people."

I said, "They had greatness in them. "

Pay it forward. "Making a Difference"

What has someone done for you in the past that you can do for someone else today? Years ago I planned to take a trip from California to Chicago, Illinois. I would fly to Chicago and take the train from the airport to my destination.

At that time, I was young and had lived in California most of my life. I was single and was much more concerned to look cute than with the weather. I never even thought about the fact that it was the middle of winter. What did I know about snow? So I arrived in Chicago wearing a darling black leather jacket and matching skirt and shoes and transferred from the airport to the train, all without stepping outside. When I arrived at the train station in downtown Chicago I was suddenly outside in 30-degree weather shivering like a chattering monkey.

> *You can give without loving, but you can never love without giving.*
> **Robert Louis Stevenson**

A lady twice my age said, "Oh my dear, you must be cold."

I was grateful she didn't say, "What in the world are you doing wearing that?" I tried a bit of a laugh and slowly said, "Yeah."

She asked, "Where are you from?"

I said, "Ca-ca-calif-for-ni-a."

She said, "No wonder you are cold." She reached into her bag and said, "Then you must take these."

She pulled out a pair of suede black gloves and handed them to me. To this day I feel like she must have been a guardian angel looking out for me.

Now I know that when the weather gets cold, go to the 99 Cent store where they have two pairs of gloves for $1, grab a bunch and give them to people who look like they need them. Believe me, the smiles they give me are way more valuable than the dollar I spent to help them.

Let's recap

*The **words of character** that resonate with me are:*
<u>Gratitude</u>, <u>Compassionate</u>, <u>Humble</u>

*What **character words** could you add about yourself?*

1._____ 2. _____ 3. _____

*The **mentor/coach** I think of is <u>Mother Teresa.</u>*

What mentor/coach do you think of? _____

Recommended Book:
The Twelfth Angel by Og Mandino

Commencements – Oprah Winfrey
http://www.youtube.com/watch?v=Bpd3raj8xww
After you watched the YouTube video, what inspired you?

Your thoughts: _____

10

Jobs, Industries, and Culture

When choosing between two similar applicants, hiring managers are increasingly turning to social media outlets to supplement information they are unable to glean from applications or interviews.

-- Amy Jo Martin

Karen Rager-Takeda   1st

President, Talent Consultant- Global Executive Recruitment Firm

Orange County, California Area | Staffing and Recruiting

Current   Rager Resources Group,LLC
Previous   Ledgent, Remedy, Beruforderung Schule
Education   Fashion Institute of Design & Merchandising

Send a message ▾

500+
connections

My Influencers: Karen Rager

What will cause a hiring manager to pick you? Do you know what a headhunter is? I thought a headhunter was a recruiter. I was wrong. Here is my lesson.

I knew a headhunter with a large practice who only worked with people who earn a quarter-of-a-million or half-a-million dollars, people like CEOs and CFOs. I went to him because he respected and admired me.

I said, "Look, I have two phenomenal friends and I'd like you to help them get a job."

He asked, "Where do they work?"

I said, "No, no, no; you must have misunderstood what I said. I have two phenomenal friends. One was a global vice-president who made about half-a-million, and the other one was a COO, and he's earning around $200,000 to a quarter-of-a-million."

> *Talent alone won't make you a success. Neither will being in the right place at the right time, unless you are ready. The most important question is: "Are you ready?"*
> **Johnny Carson**

He said, "You're not listening to me." This was definitely a breakdown in communication.

I said, "I'm sorry and I won't give any names."

He said, "I don't work with unemployed people." I finally got his point. Headhunters don't help people that need jobs; they look for strong people in secure positions who may be open to moving to another company if the right opportunity arises. Other recruiters are open to helping anyone, employed or not, find a position.

This was one of the shifts that happened for me. I said, "This is so wrong. Why wouldn't a headhunter consider a very qualified unemployed executive?" I decided to take a stand. "That's it. I'm mad."

I have 750 people in my group, Costa Mesa Connectors, on LinkedIn. We meet once a month. Rick Warren's Saddleback Church in Orange County, California sponsors a Career Night on the first Monday of each month attended by over 300 people.

I thought, "I'm going to show that headhunter that he needs to talk to unemployed people." I called over 100 people and convinced five recruiters to commit to attend my Costa Mesa Connectors event. Then I went to the Saddleback Church in South Orange County, California and passed out cards to every person at the Career Night that week that said, "Recruiters meet Job Seekers. Recruiters meet Job Seekers." I didn't get any money for this. I just did it because I was mad. How often do we ever get mad enough to take action and do something? These people at Saddleback are my friends. They deserve to have jobs.

Every recruiter that committed to attend told people, "Go ahead. Bring your resume. I promise you I will follow-up with you and work with you." Ten days later, 150 people with resumes showed up at 7 a.m. at Costa Mesa Connectors. One of the recruiters that day was Karen Rager of Rager Resources Group. She spearheaded the event and worked with these people to find employment. I met Karen at a transitional meeting for senior level managers. She is highly respected within the community and is very active in helping those less fortunate.

You are more than your resume

 Honors & Awards

Additional Honors & Awards

Loyola Marymount University Presidential Citation - 2013
Loyola Marymount University "Greek Man of the Year" Award - 2013
Fr. Alfred Kilp S.J. Service and Leadership Award - 2012
Loyola Marymount University Leadership Mention - 2011
School of Film & Television Dean's List - 2009-Current

Names, dates, employers, job description. Is this how you want someone to judge you as a person? You are much than your resume. Do you manage others? Are you involved in execution, project management, or time management? Are you involved in charities? Do you have personal hobbies that you enjoy? You are more than a two-dimensional piece of paper with your work history listed on it. In many cases, potential employers use your resume to make decisions on who gets the interview and who gets the job. If you show up as a well-rounded person with interests and passions outside work, you are much more likely to get in the door.

As you use LinkedIn and create your career and personal thread, as we started to do in the "Who am I" chapter, you realize you are so much more than your resume. The most important question becomes, "How do you match yourself with your new LinkedIn friends from all areas of your life?" Building an effective profile, making strong connections, and connecting with the right influencers can give people much more insight into who *you* are as a person, both at work and at home. As more and more recruiters and employers use LinkedIn for recruiting purposes, a good profile will put you light years ahead of potential employees who include only work-related information on their profile.

Where are the recruiters, headhunters & HR?

Recruiters, headhunters, and human resources directors are all very important people to you in your quest to find the right career. How do you find them on LinkedIn? Start with a LinkedIn search for people who use these titles in their descriptions. You will quickly identify the appropriate people for your industry. Connect with them and begin to develop a relationship with them. Connect to as many as you want. Then start to build rapport, find out what they're looking for in the perfect candidate, and examine their profile. Do your research, build a great relationship, and set yourself up for the perfect job after you finish school.

> *No occupation is so delightful to me as the culture of the earth, and no culture comparable to that of the garden.*
> **Thomas Jefferson**

Many groups on LinkedIn, if used effectively, can be instrumental in helping you find and land your dream job. Search and connect to groups in your chosen industry and then connect to the people in those groups. These connections will become extremely valuable as you look for interviews, recommendations, and networking.

Here's a bonus. I'm sharing my recruiter list of super-connectors with you. Each of these recruiters is connected to thousands of employers and can assist you in connecting the right employer for your field.

Top 12 Big Connectors - Recruiters & HR

Stacy (Berman) Birnbach | 25,000+ connections   1st
CEO/President Verus
Washington D.C. Metro Area | Staffing and Recruiting

Current   The Leukemia & Lymphoma Society, Verus Consulting Solutions, Verus Staffing Solutions
Previous   Health Search International and Clinical Resources, Health Search International, Clinical Resources Inc.
Education   University of Maryland

[Send a message] [Endorse ▼]   500+ connections

Patrick Campbell   1st
Talent Acquisition Consultant at Public Storage
Greater Los Angeles Area | Staffing and Recruiting

Current   Public Storage
Previous   Union Bank [through Collabrus], TIAA-CREF through Pride Staffing, Campbell Executive Services, Inc.
Education   Ferris State University

[Send a message] [Endorse ▼]   500+ connections

Derrick Coshow ★ Top Linked™ 21,000+   1st
Lead Technical Recruiter at Accolo
Las Vegas, Nevada Area | Staffing and Recruiting

Previous   Aristocrat, Link Technologies, Caesars Entertainment Corporation
Education   University of Nevada-Las Vegas

[Send a message] [Endorse ▼]   500+ connections

Eric Grenier 2nd

30,104+ direct connections "Top 10 Most Connected"
follow me on twitter: @comcentric

Greater Denver Area | Information Technology and Services

Current	Comcentric Inc.
Previous	RSA Companies, Profitool Inc., MW Builders / MMC Corporation
Education	University of Colorado at Denver

Connect Send Eric InMail ▼

500+
connections

Bill Gunn 1st

G&A Principal | Build Your Talent Brand | Select the
Exceptional from the Best | 23,315 Direct Connections
Top 1% Viewed

Charlotte, North Carolina Area | Management Consulting

Current	G&A
Previous	Unisys, CSC, Mitsui & Co., Ltd.
Education	Old Dominion University

Send a message Endorse ▼

500+
connections

Varsha Karnad - linkedin.varsha@gmail.com -Netwrk-22000+ 1st

Executive – Human Resources at Kraft Foods

Mumbai Area, India | Human Resources

Current	Kraft Foods - Cadbury India Ltd
Previous	Indira School Of Business Studies, ISBS - Pune, Think People Solutions Pvt Ltd
Education	Indira School Of Business Studies - ISBS

Send a message Endorse ▼

500+
connections

Phil Rosenberg 1st

LinkedIn's most connected Career Coach (30K+ 31M+),
Author http://reCareered.com, Top 20 on Linkedin globally

Greater Denver Area | Human Resources

Current	reCareered, Business Week, PersonalBranding Blog, TheLadders, CIO, Fast Company, Career Central group on Linkedin
Previous	Robert Half Management Resources, Robert Half Technology, New Horizons Computer Learning Centers
Education	Northwestern University - Kellogg School of Management

Send a message Endorse ▼

500+
connections

Ann Zaslow-Rethaber

1st

President at International Search Consultants AIRS
Diversity Certified Recruiter

Phoenix, Arizona Area | Staffing and Recruiting

Current	International Search Consultants, Inc.
Previous	Owigi Films
Education	AIRS Diversity Certified Recruiter

Send a message   Endorse ▾

500+
connections

Leonie Sands Mrep CertRP {LION 20,000+}

1st

Recruitment Consultant at Aptus Life Science

Exeter, United Kingdom | Staffing and Recruiting

Previous	Spinnaker Contract Services Limited, The Hammond Recruitment Group Ltd, Storm Recruitment
Education	University of Westminster

Send a message   Endorse ▾

500+
connections

Pete Tzavalas 1,000+(LION)

1st

Sr. Vice President at Challenger, Gray & Christmas, Inc.

petetzavalas@challengergray.com 818.536.1415

Greater Los Angeles Area | Human Resources

Current	Challenger, Gray & Christmas, Inc.
Previous	Robert Half International, Right Management, Brinks Home Security
Education	Biola University

Send a message   Endorse ▾

500+
connections

Scott Simon

1st

BetterHire Provider/Consultant 29.999 connections

Birmingham, Alabama Area | Staffing and Recruiting

Current	Betterhire.com Provider/Consulting, TechnologyAlabama.com, Access Points
Previous	Adatech Inc., National Life, National Life Group
Education	University of Alabama at Birmingham

Send a message   Endorse ▾

500+
connections

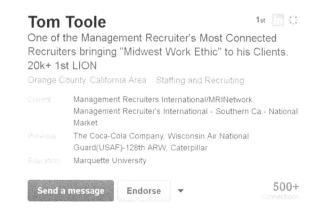

Tom Toole   1st

One of the Management Recruiter's Most Connected
Recruiters bringing "Midwest Work Ethic" to his Clients.
20k+ 1st LION

Orange County, California Area   Staffing and Recruiting

Current   Management Recruiters International/MRINetwork,
           Management Recruiter's International - Southern Ca.- National
           Market
Previous   The Coca-Cola Company, Wisconsin Air National
           Guard(USAF)-128th ARW, Caterpillar
Education Marquette University

Send a message   Endorse   ▼   500+
                                           connections

Do Your Homework

When you're interested in working for a company, you need to do your homework and research the company. Ask yourself why you would want to work for them. Take another look at the job description, review their website, and look for current events on the web. A job description tells you not just about the position you want but also gives you the voice of the company. See if their values align with yours. Check into their history, their ideals, their expectations, and investigate everything you can about the company and its hiring manager.

You can also connect with company insiders to get a sense of the corporate culture. If you are researching a public company, you can check quarterly and annual financial reports to get a feel for the challenges the company faces and the direction it is going.

Create a file for that company and add all the material that you find. Put the link to the company website in your file, create a list of key job titles, find the incumbents by searching on LinkedIn, add them to the list, review their profiles and invite them to connect. Your knowledge of your potential employer will make your interview more effective and will better equip you to understand whether the job fits your potential new career. Think of it as buying a textbook, highlighting the important lessons, identifying the takeaways, and using what you learned.

News

Leadership & Manag...
4,448,110 followers
✓ Following

Big Ideas & Innovation
3,734,135 followers
✓ Following

Technology
3,189,912 followers
✓ Following

Entrepreneurship & ...
2,826,271 followers
✓ Following

Marketing Strategies
2,723,532 followers
✓ Following

Social Media
2,341,889 followers
✓ Following

Professional Women
2,252,170 followers
✓ Following

Economy
1,905,200 followers
✓ Following

Best Advice
1,395,840 followers
✓ Following

Education
1,341,732 followers
✓ Following

Healthcare
1,244,852 followers
✓ Following

Recruiting & Hiring
1,137,566 followers
✓ Following

Positions vs. Industries

Are you searching for a position or do you want to be part of the industry? Using LinkedIn and managing your connections correctly can set you up for either. If you want to work in a given industry, connect with successful people in that industry and influencers who reflect the industry, and then network with people currently working in the industry. If you seek a position, highlight your skills, connect with leaders and mentors who can assist you in achieving your goals, and gain the recommendations needed from leaders in your field.

Let's look at a few specific industries to give you a better idea. In the banking industry, for instance, the following might come to mind when you think of banking: branch manager, teller, loan officer, commercial banking, investment banking, financial services and management, the list is endless. You can investigate, research, and entertain hundreds of positions within the banking industry. Once you identify your ideal banking position, highlight your skills, and connect to the right team.

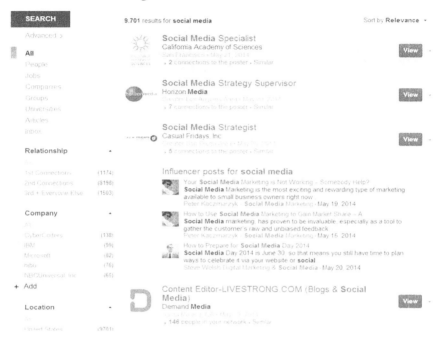

Another avenue for many is the retail industry, which is always looking for great candidates. If you don't want to work in sales, look into the corporate part of retail, including buyers, operations managers, human resources, regional managers, training departments, again the list of opportunities is endless. Search by the position you seek and begin to interact with the people who can help get you there.

The entertainment industry is also huge. Are you a performer looking to be on movie screens in front of millions of fans, a singer with fans following your concerts across the country, or do you want to act on the Broadway stage? If performing does not interest you but you want to work in the entertainment industry, you can become a director, key grip, special effects person, design costumes, be a makeup artist, or become an executive assistant, screenwriter, caterer, or one of the many thousands of people that support the team on stage. Find the industry and position you want, and then use your connections on LinkedIn to build the relationships needed to get that job.

To go deeper, if you see yourself as a leader climbing the corporate ladder, you may wonder, "How can I find that path?" Success does leave a trail and with LinkedIn you can see how mentors carve a path you can follow.

> *Culture is the process by which a person becomes all that they were created capable of being.*
> **Thomas Carlyle**

LinkedIn gives you the opportunity to see other people's success trails. On a CFO'S profile, you can see how he ended up in his current position by following his story on LinkedIn back 10, 12, or 15 years to where he or she started, perhaps as an accountant, then as a Certified Public Accountant (CPA) then controller and finally Chief Financial Officer (CFO).

Do you speak a second Language? Go International!

Are you fluent in Spanish, Italian, Farsi, Cantonese, or German? Is your primary language something other than English? Back when I was in the loan business, I led a mastermind group for a Keller Williams Real Estate office. Acquiring new business was a key challenge. I asked a group of 10 real estate agents I knew, four of whom were Hispanic, three Chinese, one Cantonese, one Persian and one Polish, "Were any of you actually born in another country?" Half of them were. Then I asked, "Do you have family in another country?" Most of them had relatives overseas. I asked them whether there were any commonalities in their last names. The girl from Poland said, "Yes, Polish names end in 'ski.'" I asked the title company if they could do a search by origin of names and they said yes. So we began to hunt.

International Groups on LinkedIn

Organization	Members
Amnesty Intl (protect Human rights worldwide)	30,000
ASIS International	59,000
BNI - Business Network International	33,000
Builders, Owners, & managers International	43,300
IFMA International Facility Management Association	28,000
IIBA International Institute of Business Analysis	60,000
International Assn of Business communicators	32,000
International baccalaureate	25,000
International Business	71,000
International Coast Fed (Sustainable Development)	40,000
International Council of Shopping Centers	39,000
International Freight	28,000
International Import/Export	129,000
International Network for the Arts (Theater and art)	23,000
International Relations Professionals	30,000
International relations/Affairs	30,000
International School Educators	21,000
International Society for Technology/Education	41,000
International sports	27,000
International Trade	56,000
International TV Professionals	57,000
Jobs in NGOS	27,000
Sustainable Green	30,000
Technical Assistance Consultancy Network	34,000
Toastmasters International	36,000
Zezex (International Development)	47,000

If you know 100 people who know you, like you, and trust you, you have all the connections you need. This is especially true if you speak a foreign language. A former colleague, a bank branch manager, who spoke Farsi and had the biggest book of business in Orange County, put this idea to use when she advertised for business in Los Angeles. She attracted half her clientele from Los Angeles because many of them were more comfortable speaking their native language when they did business.

One of the challenges for any retail organization is communicating with people from different backgrounds. Another friend of mine managed a home improvement store in Los Angeles located in an area where Chinese-speaking individuals lived. Very few of them shopped at his store. To change that pattern, my friend found an employee who spoke Chinese and assigned him the mission of getting his Chinese friends to shop at the store. As an added inducement, he was to be their personal shopper so they would feel comfortable when they arrived. The associate she picked was a special needs employee with a job coach. When his manager put him on his new task as Chinese Lead Generator, his eyes lit up and he was excited every time a new customer came to him for help. He became a needed individual in the store and was called on by all departments to assist in translation. It changed the way he looked at his job when he became a valued member of the team. Sales increased as more and more Chinese-speaking customers visited the store.

If you go on LinkedIn and put the word "Spanish" in the search engine and select "people," you will find over 4,546,000 names.

Polish people add 257,757, Chinese account for 1,115,000, and Italians 1,195,000. Continue your search in your native language or secondary language and you'll find thousands of individuals who share that language with you. Be sure to add all the languages you speak and your proficiency to your profile so those searching for speakers of other languages can find you easily.

If you search the word "International" on LinkedIn you will find 19,000 results. From financial services, IT, accounting, computer software, to management consultants, people around the world are connecting to each other. You will find 46,000 international groups on LinkedIn including fashion, import and export trade, freight, television professionals, Beta Gamma Sigma honor society, and Toastmasters International. LinkedIn makes doing business on a global level easier.

The chart on page 129 shows you how many members many of the international groups on LinkedIn have.

Organizational chart: Who connects to who?

When researching a new company, one of the best things to use, if you can get it, is their organizational chart. This will show you how the company is organized and who is connected and how.

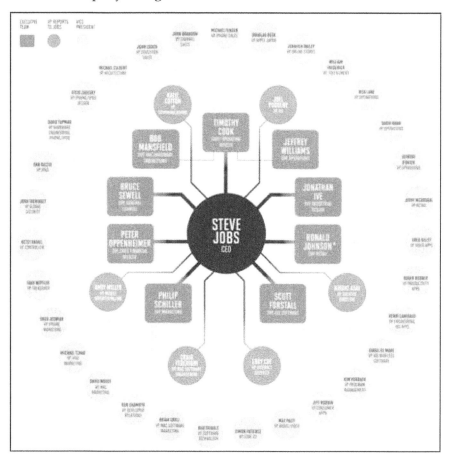

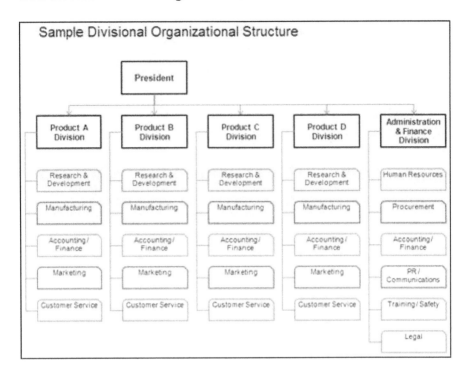

People hire People for Jobs

I have heard time after time that, "It's not the grade, it's not the GPA, it's the attitude." Whether he or she is CEO of the company or Director of HR, the hiring manager will always choose the best fit for the culture of their organization. In a research company, this could mean the best person is one who knows how to research in a creative way. In a sales position, they're looking for a relationship builder, an ambassador position, for a person with credibility. They hire you because of your character, your values, and your integrity. They hire you as a person.

I am convinced that nothing we do is more important than hiring and developing people. At the end of the day you bet on people, not on strategies.

Larry Bossidy

How do you effectively align yourself or find the right people that will introduce you to the right people? Here's where using LinkedIn in an effective manner can be of great benefit! Once your profile is built with authenticity and transparency, you've started building relationships and connections with your top 100 as well as their top 100's, and you've done your research on your top five companies, it will all fall into place. You will be aligned with the right people. They will know your character and potential because of the relationship you have built with them. As you research the companies and people within those companies, your network will assist you in making the connections and aligning yourself.

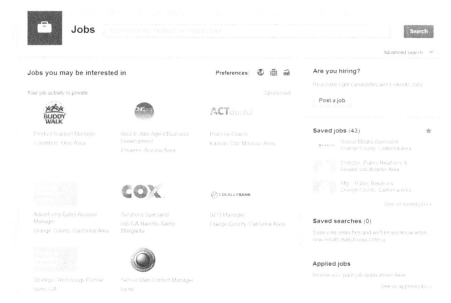

Non-Profits are Jobs too

After a conversation with Jim Palmer one day, I looked on LinkedIn and discovered that over 6,000 people had Non-Profit in their profile. While looking for opportunities in the career world, do not neglect non-profit organizations. These organizations represent amazing causes and hire people with all sorts of knowledge.

People in Your Top Five Companies

You've done it. You've come to the end of your college career and now you're ready to take on the world. You have completed your major, finished your research, and know what you want to do. How do you find that job?

If you have created your profile on LinkedIn and have done your homework and research as I've shown you, you will be well on your way. As you look at companies and opportunities, begin to identify the most important people in the companies you're searching.

Industry List from LinkedIn

Accounting	Airlines/Aviation
Alternative Dispute Resolution	Alternative Medicine
Animation	Apparel & Fashion
Architecture & Planning	Arts & Crafts
Automotive	Aviation & Aerospace
Banking	Biotechnology
Broadcast Media	Building Materials
Business Supplies, Equipment	Capital Markets
Chemicals	Civic & Social Organization
Civil Engineering	Commercial Real Estate
Computer & Network Security	Computer Games
Computer Hardware	Computer Software
Construction	Consumer Electronics
Consumer Goods	Consumer Services
Cosmetics	Dairy
Defense & Space	Design
Education Management	E-Learning
Electronic Manufacturing	Entertainment
Environmental Services	Event Services
Executive Offices	Facilities Services
Farming	Financial Services
Fine Art	Fisheries
Food & Beverages	Food Production
Fund-Raising	Furniture
Gambling & Casinos	Glass, Ceramics, & Concrete
Government Administration	Government Relations

Graphic Design	Health, Wellness & Fitness
Higher Education	Hospital & Health Care
Hospitality	Human Resources
Import & Export	Individual & Family Services
Industrial Automation	Information Services
International Affairs	Insurance
Information Technology and Services	International Trade & Development
Internet	Investment Banking
Investment Management	Judiciary
Law Enforcement	Law Practice
Legal Services	Legislative Office
Leisure, Travel, & Tourism	Libraries
Logistics & Supply Chain	Luxury Goods & Jewelry
Machinery	Management Consulting
Maritime	Marketing and Advertising
Market Research	Mechanical Engineering
Media Production	Medical Devices
Medical Practice	Mental Health Care
Military	Mining & Metals
Motion Pictures & Films	Museums & Institutions
Music	Nanotechnology
Newspapers	Nonprofit Organization Mgmt
Oil & Energy	Online Media
Outsourcing/Offshoring	Package/Freight Delivery
Packaging & Containers	Paper & Forest Products
Performing Arts	Pharmaceuticals
Philanthropy	Photography
Plastics	Political Organization
Primary/Secondary Education	Printing
Professional Trainer and Coach	Program Development
Public Policy	PR and Communications
Public Safety	Publishing
Railroad Manufacture	Ranching
Real Estate	Recreational Facilities & Services
Religious Institutions	Renewables and Environment

Research	Restaurants
Retail	Security and Investigations
Semiconductors	Shipbuilding
Sporting Goods	Sports
Staffing & Recruiting	Supermarkets
Telecommunications	Textiles
Think Tanks	Tobacco
Translation & Localization	Transportation/Trucking/Railroad
Utilities	Venture Capital and Private Equity
Veterinary	Warehousing
Wholesale	Wine and Spirits
Wireless	Writing and Editing

Select your top five companies, those that align with your planned career, and, using the search bar, search for people whose profiles have those company names. Read their profiles and connect with them. Build the relationships, research their profiles, and begin to understand your Top Five companies, not from the business side, which you have already done, but from the people side. Get a feel for the people who make up the companies. Let them get to know you! They need you as much as you need them.

> *You can't connect the dots looking forward; you can only connect them looking backwards. So you have to trust that the dots will somehow connect in your future.*
> **Steve Jobs**

Let's recap

*The **words of character** that resonate with me are:*
Imagination, Knowledge, Genius

*What **character words** could you add about yourself?*

1._____ 2. _____ 3. _____

*The **mentor/coach** I think of is Albert Einstein.*

What mentor/coach do you think of? _____

Recommended Book:
Confessions of a Recruiting Director by Brad Karsh

Commencements – Steve Jobs
http://www.youtube.com/watch?v=UF8uR6Z6KLc

After you watched the YouTube video, what inspired you?

Your thoughts: _____

11

Success Leaves a Trail

I am telling you to make a choice based on your passions and interests, not what everyone else is telling you to do. It doesn't work that way. You wind up living a life for the wrong reasons, and you never get the most out of it. Just always think about why you are doing what you are doing.

Jeff Hoffman

Eli Davidson   1st

Executive Coach, Business Speaker Media: The Today Show, CNN & New York Times

Greater Los Angeles Area   Professional Training & Coaching

Current	The Huffington Post, The Davidson Partnership Corp. The Today Show, The Davidson Partnership
Previous	WE tv (AMC Networks), CNN, National Speakers Association
Education	University of Santa Monica

Send a message   Endorse ▼

500+
connections

My Influencers: Eli Davidson

As elegant as the lace on Princess Diana's wedding dress, Eli Davidson is a vision of perfection. I met Eli in the lobby of the Westin Hotel near LAX international airport in Los Angeles, California. She was dressed immaculately and gave the appearance of a woman on a mission. She looked at me briefly as she stood at the counter and then turned away. I instantly felt a vibration, almost as if someone had called my name. She turned around again and this time I couldn't help but to ask her why she was here. She responded, "I am here on business."

I replied, "I feel like I know you."

> Coming together is a beginning;
> keeping together is a progress;
> Working together is success.
> **Henry Ford**

"We were destined to meet today," she said. We found a couch close by and began to chat like long-lost friends.

I said, "I feel like a little kid I'm so excited to meet you. Tell me more about you and what is exciting in your life."

I wasn't quite ready for her response. "I coach celebrities like Joan Rivers," she said. "I also put on live events helping authors; Speakers and entrepreneurs find their diamond niche. Why you are here?"

"I'm here for the College Speaker Boot Camp that James Malinchak puts on. He helps speakers and authors create business strategies," I said. "I'm writing a book on LinkedIn to help students who spent four to eight years in college to get the skills to get a job. Even after that many years, they haven't built the right relationships and connections that will help them get the jobs that they went to school to get.

One thing led to another and before I knew it I was her LinkedIn coach and on a plane to Las Vegas to see her "Live" at her "Be On Stage" event. My time with this lovely woman was down to earth and very connective. I wasn't surprised that, as I watched her live on stage, she connected with the 500 people in her audience with the same gift of authenticity she used when she connected with me. First she shared her humble beginnings in a little farm town in Kansas, just like Dorothy in the *Wizard of Oz*. She followed her yellow brick road in her first business venture but lost everything. She calls herself "Strappy," so she pulled herself up from there by her bootstraps, used a $17 glue gun to build "Elizabeth Davidson

Design," and created a company that generated $1,500,000 in retail sales and became the author of the book *Funky to Fabulous*, in which she shows how games and fun are integral to learning and to transforming your life.

As the event continued, Eli showed the audience the top-gun strategies she used to dream the dream, align with the right people, and take the steps needed to grow her company. Then she brought to the stage, one by one, Super Power People who shared their specific expertise with the audience. Finally, she introduced her secret guest speaker and mentor Jeff Hoffman, the Founder of PriceLine.com. "Seriously," I asked myself, "what would it take to get a mentor who had created a billion-dollar company?" I felt so honored and blessed that she shared her humbleness with me and let me be part of her life.

> *Only one thing...a desire so strong, a determination so intense, that you cheerfully throw everything you have into the scale to win what you want. Not merely your work and your money and your thought, but the willingness to stand or fall by the result — to do or to die.*
> **Robert Collier**

During your college career, you have already met many people who could help you as you search for your first job in the corporate world. Just as important is to be open to unexpected meetings with people who might become a great influence on your life. Always keep that gift of curiosity, the desire to know more about them and how they got there.

Looking outside the box

Thinking outside the box is a key to success. When you are creative as you approach your career, you will find solutions and answers others won't bother to seek out for themselves.

Earlier in this book I showed you that questions are the answer. If you understand this aphorism, it will change your world. It's not what you know that's important; it's what you don't know that you need to know that will be critical to your success. Ask yourself questions about where you want to work and what type of work you want to do. Then dig for solutions. Use LinkedIn to help in your quest for your career after college. You will have millions of people, industries, jobs, and employers at your fingertips. Use your ingenuity and the relationships that you've built find new solutions to old problems. Could an internship lead to a career? What about this summer job will help me get the career I desire? If I reach out to the CEO, will he answer me? These are a few examples of questions you can ask yourself to begin thinking outside the box and setting up your life in the manner you desire.

> *If you're trying to achieve, there will be roadblocks. I've had them; everybody has had them. But obstacles don't have to stop you. If you run into a wall, don't around and give up. Figure out how to climb it, go through it, or work around it.*
> **Michael Jordan**

When you search for your first job after graduation, LinkedIn gives you a detailed roadmap that will guide you through the maze of companies where you could play your desired role.

Questions are the Answer

When I go to an event, I always ask myself what the most important thing I learned was. At a Tony Robbins seminar 20 years ago, I learned a set of questions and a mindset that I still use today: What is your purpose, what is your intention, and questions are the answers.

Here's how you do it differently. You ask yourself, "What's my purpose and what's my intention?" Your answer might be, "My purpose is to meet people I can build relationships with that further my purpose to find a job for a client."

Is that part of your intention? No. Your intention might be, "I'm going to look for ways in which I can better serve my clients so I've compiled a list of 20 things I did in the past that didn't help my clients."

> *Discipline is the bridge between goals and accomplishment.*
> **Jim Rohn**

When you do this, ask, "What are the questions that I can ask a person attending this event?" That would be far more productive. One of Stephen Covey's most important mindsets is, "First seek to understand then to be understood." If you invest in the people you want to meet and help and not in your own story, you will be far more successful.

Recently, I transformed a client's job-seeking world from networking for two years with no success to getting a job within 60 days. Here is how I did it. I asked an audience, "How many of you go to networking events?" I knew the answer. They all raised their hands and said they network. The error they make is that networking is not the end; it's a means to the end. It gives you the opportunity to meet people and build relationships. True networking results from qualifying and building the relationships you start at the networking event.

Questions are the answer to your problems. They are everything. No matter where you go, it is all about the questions. If your intention is find members of your market, start asking questions that will draw the people you are trying to attract to you.

When Tony Robbins taught me about questions and answers, he instilled in me the idea that we have to ask the right questions of ourselves and of others to get the best possible answers. When you do this right, you will forge the strongest possible relationships with others and with yourself.

The best investment you can make in yourself is getting to know yourself. Read books, take risks, and get involved in clubs that will teach you leadership. There you will discover the skills you do and do not possess and which skills you must acquire.

Jack Canfield says, "Everything you want in life is just outside your comfort zone." Step outside your normal circle of friends, your normal habits, and your normal cycle. Stretch yourself and then ask yourself how the experience felt. Analyze it by asking yourself if it made you feel inferior in some areas and superior in others. By doing this you learn and grow. You can then bring these lessons to the table when you go on interviews or sales calls.

What is ROI vs. ROT

In the finance and investment world, everyone thinks return on your investment (ROI). In the networking world, people will network and network and have nothing to show for the time invested. They neglect that most important metric, Return on Your Time (ROT).

In Chapter 5, I mentioned how I transformed a friend's job seeking world from networking for two years with no results to getting a job within 60 days. Here's the full story.

Since I know a lot of people who don't take their networking to a deep enough level or qualify the time spent against the results achieved, I quickly recognized his problem.

I asked my friend, "How many networking events do you go to a week?"

He answered, "Five to seven."

I asked him, "What does your wife say when you get home?"

He answered, "She asks me how it went."

I asked, "And your reply?"

"Okay."

"*Wow!*" I said. "Let's do the math. Say you attend three events a week and it takes you an hour and half to get ready and to drive there. Is that fair?"

He said, "Yes."

I said, "You probably spend at least an hour and a half, right? That's about 12 hours a week looking for a job, and you only worked with three events."

This shows that with an effective profile on LinkedIn and connections in place, you can reach hundreds of companies in a short period of time. With recommendations from former colleagues and bosses, influencers who share your vision, and endorsements for your skills, potential employers will get a feel for who you are, to what you're committed and whether you're a good fit for their organization or not. In the current job market, as in every past era, the best way to get a job is to find a connection with more celebrity in your field than you have who can promote you inside a company or who has connections inside the company.

Internet searches and posting resumes to hundreds of companies has become a thing of the past. Using your connections and resources is the way to get your next job. Through the networking and profiling available on LinkedIn, you will be ahead of the others out there searching for a career.

Strategize your Success

When McDonald's spends a million dollars to build a new store, they position it carefully, on a corner if possible, near an intersection if they can, so it is easily visible to oncoming traffic. If you sit at a traffic light for one or two minutes, your brain may notice a McDonald's down the road and say, "McDonald's! I'm hungry!"

> *Winners never quit and quitters never win.*
> **Vince Lombardi**

Many times people find themselves in the parking lot of a McDonald's or other fast food place they had no intention of visiting. Very few of them leave the house saying, "I'm going to McDonald's today," but they wind up there anyway.

In the same way, some people know that if they plan to eat a healthy lunch, they need to pack their lunch; which means planning ahead and buying healthy foods. When people make this commitment, they know what their bodies need and make health a high level value.

Both of these examples represent a strategic plan. McDonald's uses strategy to place its restaurants in the right spot to get people to stop. The person who packs their lunch uses a different strategy. To succeed in college or life, you too must adopt a strategy.

The same thing happens on LinkedIn. To be successful using LinkedIn you must adopt a strategy. Yours may differ from your roommate's. Start with the end in mind, work backwards and let LinkedIn work for you. Use the strategies I have outlined in this book to build a plan to connect with the best people in your industry, develop local and the national celebrity connections, use those connections to get in the door, then let your knowledge and ideas sine in the interview that will land you your ideal job.

Who's Your Wingman?

One of my favorite movies from the 80's, *Top Gun,* depicts this next concept very nicely. The movie pairs Maverick, an egotistical fighter pilot, with Goose, his co-pilot/navigator. The two are inseparable. They compete with another pair of aviators at the top of their game as well, led by Iceman. Maverick and Iceman are rivals who don't care for each other. They have extremely different styles, different agendas, and clash at every opportunity. By the end of the movie, the two have resolved their differences and come to acknowledge that each has valuable skills. One of the best lines comes from Maverick after they've engaged in a dogfight with enemy aircraft. He looks at Ice and says, "You can be my wingman any time." Ice responds with, "No, you can be mine!" It shows

Smart phones and social media expand our universe. We can connect with others or collect information easier and faster than ever.
Daniel Goleman

that the two have figured out how to work together and to succeed.

Your wingman is a person you can count on, who is willing to take great risks for you, and who will ensure that you reach your ultimate goal. Who is your wingman? Like Maverick and Ice, you may start out rocky, but develop a bond that is strong and able to withstand anything. Develop strong, lasting relationships through LinkedIn and you will find that your wingmen will help you get the job you seek.

Can Social Media be Social Business?

There's a misconception that LinkedIn isn't social media and can be used only as a business network. However, like Facebook, LinkedIn is used to connect with others and start conversations and is an acceptable form of social media.

People have been in the business of being social since business began. From playing golf with doctors to weekend cocktail parties at the office, the social aspect is a huge part of business. With the addition

Social media is an amazing tool, but it's really the face-to-face interaction that makes a long-term impact.
Felicia Day

of the Internet, social interactions have stepped onto a whole new platform and expanded to include multi-media sites that make it easier than ever to reach people globally. Each platform has its strengths in different industries and genres. Some of my friends on different platforms are highly successful business people.

John Chow   1st
Founder & CEO at TTZ Media, Inc.
Vancouver, Canada Area   Internet

Current   TTZ Media Inc., John Chow dot Com, TTZ Media. Inc.

Send a message   Endorse   ▼   500+
                                                                        connections

We all know how popular blogging has become. From Fortune 500 companies to our favorite health television show, Dr. Oz, everyone is blogging or reading blogs, most of them on WordPress.

My favorite blogger is my friend John Chow, who I have lunch with on a regular basis and whose daughter plays with my dog from time to time. John talks about everyday stuff on his blog. Several times, I've seen him post photos of his lunch on his blog.

Joel Comm
1st

New York Times Best-Selling Author | International Keynote Speaker | Entrepreneur | New Media Marketing Strategist

Greater Denver Area   Information Technology and Services

Current	Joel Comm, Inc., a Joel Comm Company	International Conference & Keynote Speaker	Corporate Events, InfoMediaInc.com, a Joel Comm Company; Joel Comm is an International Public Keynote Speaker
Previous	Digital Future, Inc., a Joel Comm Company; Joel is an international motivational speaker, ClassicGames.com	Acquired by Yahoo as Yahoo! Games (Joel is now a keynote & motivational speaker)
Education	University of Illinois at Urbana-Champaign

Send a message   500+

In the Twitter world, blogging is content driven with short and sweet tweets, tiny snippets ending with a hash tag or a link. Twitter is very popular in the job world. Joel Com uses Twitter very effectively for his business. In the Google Plus world they love their Google hangouts and You Tube.

Jack C Crawford
1st

Senior Director at Cognizant Technology Solutions ∴ Advisory Consultant, Customer Solutions Practice

Greater Los Angeles Area   Information Technology and Services

Current	Cognizant Technology Solutions
Previous	Allergan, 2-1-1 Orange County, OC Partnership to End Homelessness
Education	Claremont Graduate University

Send a message   500+

My dear friend Jack Crawford uses Google Plus regularly and speaks to and interviews many people through Google Hangouts. Mia Voss uses Google Hangouts for interviews and meetings. You can use your media link from You Tube to post interviews for Google Hangout on your LinkedIn profile.

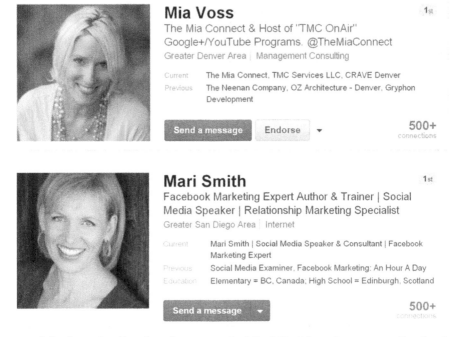

Mia Voss 1st

The Mia Connect & Host of "TMC OnAir"
Google+/YouTube Programs. @TheMiaConnect
Greater Denver Area | Management Consulting

Current   The Mia Connect, TMC Services LLC, CRAVE Denver
Previous   The Neenan Company, OZ Architecture - Denver, Gryphon Development

[Send a message]   [Endorse]   ▼   **500+** connections

Mari Smith 1st

Facebook Marketing Expert Author & Trainer | Social Media Speaker | Relationship Marketing Specialist
Greater San Diego Area | Internet

Current   Mari Smith | Social Media Speaker & Consultant | Facebook Marketing Expert
Previous   Social Media Examiner, Facebook Marketing: An Hour A Day
Education   Elementary = BC, Canada; High School = Edinburgh, Scotland

[Send a message]   ▼   **500+** connections

My favorite Facebook person is Mari Smith, who wrote *Facebook for Dummies*.

As we move further into the twenty-first century, the internet will continue to become more and more a way to communicate, network, and build relationships. Although each site is designed with a specific purpose, in general they all work to connect people and share communications with others.

Let's recap

*The **words of character** that resonate with me are:*
Entrepreneur, Resourcefulness, Reciprocity

*What **character words** could you add about yourself?*

1._____ 2. _____ 3. _____

*The **mentor/coach** I think of is Thomas Edison.*

What mentor/coach do you think of? _____

Recommended Book:
Becoming a Person of Influence by John Maxwell

Commencements – Reid Hoffman
http://www.youtube.com/watch?v=3turaJ_QsNo

After you watched the YouTube video, what inspired you?

Your thoughts: _____

12

B4U Graduate,
Build Your Future

Success comes from taking the initiative and following up...
persisting... eloquently expressing the depth of your love. What
simple action could you take today to produce a new momentum
toward success in your life?
--Tony Robbins

Jerome Carter   1st

Owner, Inspiration 52 and Education Management
Consultant

Greater Los Angeles Area | Education Management

Current   A.C. Media Productions, Inspiration 52
Previous   Loyola Mary Mount University, Los Angeles Unified School
               District
Education   California State University-Dominguez Hills; Long Beach State
               Universit Find other members who attended California State University-Dominguez Hills; Long Beach State University

| Send a message | Endorse ▾ | **500+**
                                          connections

My Influencers: Jerome Carter

I met Jerome Carter at an event for Keynote College Speakers a
few years ago. During one of the lunch breaks I had the opportunity
to speak with Jerome and find out more about him. As we were

150

talking, I asked him if he had a mentor. Jerome answered quickly that James Malinchak was his mentor in the realm of college speaking. He paused for a second, looked at me and said, "My real mentor was my dad." This is one of the most important lessons he gives to college students. Jerome views his dad as a man of integrity, loyalty, friendship, patience, confidence, and love who taught him most of what he considers important in life.

Jerome uses the lessons he learned in his life to help and inspire others. His company, Inspiration 52, teaches character education through principles and inspirational poetry. Jerome empowers high school students to develop their own character, leadership, and creative self-expression. He believes that "just because you went through crap, doesn't mean your life and future are crap."

> *If your actions inspire others to dream more, learn more, do more and become more, you are a leader.*
> **John Quincy Adams**

Jerome told me that he grew up in a gang-infested neighborhood and never thought he'd make it past age 17. In college, he changed his major four times before graduating. His message for college students is that it's okay not to know what's coming next. Take life as it comes and do your very best, no matter what job you have. He tells others to "Never let your past predict your future." He adds, "My objective is to do my part to make this world a better place for all those that I have the privilege of encountering."

Coaches, Mentors & Role Models

When we develop habits, those habits control our destiny. This is why people who make millions of dollars are willing to pay a coach a thousand dollars a month without thinking anything of it to keep themselves on track, taking the actions they commit to taking.

Building these habits starts in college and even before. That's why one of the best things a student could do is hire a coach to keep him on track as he builds the academic record that will make him a prime candidate for jobs after graduation. You need this coaching support because it is so easy to get sidetracked when you're not supported by a structure that tells you what to do every day.

> *The price of success is hard work, dedication to the job at hand, and the determination that whether we win or lose, we have applied the best of ourselves to the task at hand.*
> **Vince Lombardi**

One of my favorite people to go to lunch with during events is Kory Minor. I met Kory a few years back and had no idea who he was. At a college speaking event, we bumped into each other and talked for a few minutes. I realized he was charming, funny, and down to earth.

I asked him, "What did you do in your previous life?"

He responded, "I was a linebacker and special teams player for the San Francisco 49ers."

I was so excited because I'm from the Bay area. As we talked, I asked Kory what he was most proud of in his life. He said that he was a blessed man because he received a full scholarship to Notre Dame University. He played football for the Irish and got an amazing education. We then moved on to Kory's mentor, Les Brown, who coincidentally is one of my mentors and one of my favorite people.

I asked him, "How and why did you make the transition from football to speaker?"

He thought for a moment and then said, "Everybody gets knocked down and we all have to get back up. Not everybody has an easy childhood and some of us come from the wrong side of the tracks. But everyone fights adversity."

Kory explained that his biggest fear is the fear of failure. He had a strong desire to create his own legacy and a dream of becoming an entrepreneur. Kory is the Founder and CEO of Kory Minor

Industries (www.koryminor.com) which is a personal development and training company working with individuals and organizations to "get off the sideline and get into the game." He has written the book *Make a Touchdown of Your Life* and believes that you have greatness inside you. Kory says there are four pieces to the success puzzle:

1. Have a game plan
2. Take action
3. Fight through adversity
4. Be adaptable

Kory sees life as a vessel to help others. He believes that if you have the right play and follow the right steps you can make a touchdown of your life. Kory's big goal is to teach teenagers financial literacy. He believes that smart people use their brains make a difference.

Les Brown is one of my favorite mentors. He has worked with many generations and inspired many people. When you watch Les Brown speak you can feel the energy he generates. He is filled with passion and gives deep, emotional speeches. At one point, I had the opportunity to have dinner with him. A friend invited me

> *Good leadership consists of showing average people how to do the work of superior people.*
> **John D. Rockefeller**

to meet up with her and it turns out that her husband was getting private coaching from Les Brown. They invited me to dinner and it was such an honor to have dinner with one of my greatest role models. There were just 10 of us there and it is an experience I will never forget.

Honors, Interns, and Innovators

You entered college with great GPA and became part of the honors program at your school. Attending special classes, being included in extra workshops, participating in high level clubs all worked to help you gain an advantage in school and that advantage will continue as you enter the work force. As you've seen in this book, employers hire great character. As an honor student, the work ethic you've demonstrated thus far in school will help launch you into the career world. You have shown that you're not afraid to be one of the best and are willing to go the extra mile. Employers are looking for people with your work ethic.

As you go through college, many opportunities will present themselves and many choices will arise. One of the best opportunities is for you to take advantage of an internship. Doing an internship in the field that you're interested in will give you great insight and valuable work experience. After working side by side with people already in your field, you can determine if you've made the right choice, that this career is right for you. You can find

> *When you believe you can*
> *– you can!*
> **Maxwell Maltz**

Internship opportunities everywhere. A few examples are: medical offices, medical laboratories, dentist office, veterinary office, Google, environmental science, a newspaper or blog, programming. The list goes on and on. If you are considering entering a certain field, it is worth your time to do an internship there. There's nothing better than on the job training.

Dell, SalesForce.com, Facebook, Microsoft. What do these companies have in common? They all started in someone's garage or on the kitchen table. They were formed by entrepreneurs who used their pioneer spirit and creative ideas to create new and different companies. They took a chance and believed they could create something of their own. Many of these companies agreed to make products and signed contracts before they even had their prototype completed. They believed they had an idea and they followed their heart to make it happen. Just like Ford with the first Model-T, their determination, persistence, and drive made them successful. They had the courage to try something new and the persistence to stay with it until it worked. You too have that same opportunity if you desire. Do you have the next great idea? Are you willing to give it all you have and see your dream through to a reality?

No matter which direction you take in life, working for an established company or creating one out of your garage, by using your character traits and skills, adding your passion and drive, and giving it your all, you will become successful in anything you choose.

How the Internet Changed Education

In today's world, information is at your fingertips. Want to find a place to eat? Search for one and within a minute you will have more choices than you know what to do with.

> *Leadership is the art of getting someone else to do something you want done because he wants to do it.*
> **Dwight D. Eisenhower**

The internet has also changed the way we learn. We have developed technologies and systems that extend education to a larger group of people. Online classes for people of all ages are becoming more and more popular. Changes are coming so fast with the internet that not only is education available, education companies are finding ways to increase and improve the outcomes that internet education can deliver.

In 2004 Salman Kahn began posting math tutorial videos on You Tube. From these videos, he developed the Kahn Academy, a carefully structured series of educational videos offering complete curricula originally in math but now in additional subjects as well. He teaches through the videos and shows the power of interactive exercises. He's flipping the current education model and asks teachers to create video lectures the students can watch at home while doing homework in class where they can ask questions and get help.

The teachers that use Kahn's videos are using technology to humanize the classroom. The one size fits all lectures are gone, replaced by students interacting with one another to learn. One of Kahn's biggest supporters in this new form of education is Bill Gates. The Kahn Academy is a non-profit organization with significant funding from the Bill & Melinda Gates Foundation, Ann and John Doer, Lemann Foundation, and Google.

In addition to new ways of learning, students have access to more information than ever before. Projects and reports that used to be taxing have become much simpler due to the internet. Articles and books are online and easily accessible. Knowledge is at everyone's fingertips. You just have to step out and search for it.

Creating Visualizations

John Assaraf   1st

CEO, PraxisNow | Built 5 Multi-Million Dollar Companies | Philanthropist | NY Times Best Selling Author

Rancho Santa Fe, California   Professional Training & Coaching

Current   PraxisNow
Previous   RIA Ventures, Inc., IPIX Corporation, RE/MAX of Indiana
Education   Montreal Canada

Send a message   Endorse ▾   500+ connections

In the movie *The Secret*, there's a scene where John Assaraf had just moved into his new home and was unpacking boxes in his office. His son walked in to help him unpack. He pulled a large board with pictures and words pasted on it out of a box. "Wow, my old vision board," he said. "It's been years since I looked at this."

"What's a vision board, Dad?" his son asked.

"A vision board is a place where you put your dreams," he said. "You write down or add photos of the stuff you want to accomplish and it helps you work toward it."

He opened the box and pulled out the vision board that he had created five years earlier. As he turned the board around his son gasped. There on the board was a photo of the house they had just moved into. Five years earlier, John had put his house on the vision board, and his vision had just come true. What a coincidence.

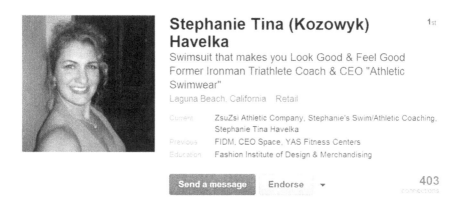

Stephanie Tina (Kozowyk) Havelka

1st

Swimsuit that makes you Look Good & Feel Good
Former Ironman Triathlete Coach & CEO "Athletic Swimwear"
Laguna Beach, California   Retail

Current   ZsuZsi Athletic Company, Stephanie's Swim/Athletic Coaching, Stephanie Tina Havelka
Previous   FIDM, CEO Space, YAS Fitness Centers
Education   Fashion Institute of Design & Merchandising

Send a message   Endorse   ▾

403
connections

Recently I stayed at my friend Stephanie's house in Laguna Niguel, California, just south of Los Angeles, for the weekend. When I arrived, she met me at the door and said, "I got you a spot under the stars."

"What do you mean?" I replied.

"I got you a spot under the stars. Follow me." We headed down the hall to an amazing room with huge windows and a soft fluffy bed piled with pillows. I thought, "This is amazing." Then I looked up and saw stars above my head. I thought I was in heaven!

After a night of wonderful dreams in an amazing room under the stars, I woke up refreshed. I looked around and on her bookshelf I saw John Assaraf's book, *The Vision Board Book*. What a coincidence. John Assaraf and I had connected through LinkedIn.

My friend Stephanie arrived and saw me with the book. "I see you got into my books," she said.

"I'm a book nut. I love this book and John Assaraf is one of my connections on LinkedIn." I then shared the story of the vision board and the house with Stephanie.

"I'm in that book," she said.

"No way!" I said.

"I'm in that book," she said again.

Again, I said, "No way!"

"I'm in that book. There's a story about how I trained to compete in the Ironman Competition."

It finally sunk in. My friend Stephanie was actually in this book! She told me the whole story. She had done several triathlons and had just finished a race in Boston. Shortly after that race, she received a call informing her that she had qualified for the Ironman Competition in Hawaii. This worldwide competition has only 1,500 spots available. She had just qualified for one of those spots. They needed one question answered immediately, "Are you in or will you pass?"

An answer right now, she thought, okay, when opportunity knocks just say yes. So she said yes. She had just committed to this event, but then realized she had no idea what she had committed to.

> *Failure is the opportunity to more intelligently begin again.*
> **Henry Ford**

What was an Ironman? Where was it? When was it? She had no clue that she had just committed herself to an Ironman competition in Hawaii in 45 days.

Once she figured out that it was a triathlon that included three events, a 2.4-mile swim, a 112-mile bike race, and a 26.2-mile marathon, she realized she had to do something drastic.

She had never done anything remotely like this. Most athletes train for the Ironman for a year or two. She had 45 days. So she went to the one person she knew who could help her, a friend who trained athletes on visualization. This friend agreed to help her train for her Ironman and they began with very specific drills and training for both the mind and body. She had to condition her mind to see the end result before she could get her body in shape in 45 days. She focused on seeing herself in the race, seeing her body in condition for the race, and felt herself running the race.

The power of our mind, the biggest muscle we possess, is incredible. She performed a successful Ironman because she stayed focused and trained her mind to get her to where she needed to be physically.

Renee Piane   1st
Design the Life you Want with Vision Boards, Author, Speaker, Matchmaker, TV Celebrity, Love Designer
Greater Los Angeles Area   Entertainment

Current   www.SinglesAdvice.com, Renee Piane Enterprises LLC - Rapid Dating & Networking, Various Matchmaking Companies

Send a message   Endorse   ▼   500+
                                                      connections

Like your profile has a trajectory of its own, so will your networking experiences. As I shared eWomenNetwork meetings, the more I met people with goals common to mine.

One time I was sitting at a table getting acquainted when I overheard this lady talking about a raffle prize she was giving away, a *Create your Vision Board* class. I perked up, turned around, and said, "I couldn't help but hear you talk about the vision board."

I love mind mapping, goal setting, and vision boards. The coincidences and connections that result are amazing. This awareness is a prime characteristic of successful people.

If you want to be successful, find someone who has achieved the results you want and copy what they do and you'll achieve the same results.

Tony Robbins

Renee Piane has helped people find their dream home, more clients, and soul-mates. She claims her secret to success in meeting her client's desires is to make them concrete with a visual anchor, very much as in Napoleon Hill's book *Think and Grow Rich*, where he shows you how to mix desire with emotion to create the goal and the vision.

Mind mapping puts the ideas into a time line, where you break down your goals and add in numbers, details, and strategies to meet them. Renee is living proof. She manifested her amazing husband Joe and her adorable dog Buddy with vision board where the images of a man and a dog mirrored future reality.

Billion Dollar Mindset and Game Changers

One of my favorite people from *The Secret* is John D. Martini. John mentioned that *The Secret* told a lot of great stories about universal laws but he adds the action steps needed to get to the end in mind. This process is how billionaires make their billions of dollars.

One billionaire he talks about is Warren Buffet. People wonder how successful people become successful. At age 11 Warren Buffet read every book on finance in the Nebraska State Library in Omaha. No wonder Warren Buffet is worth $50 billion dollars. This Billionaire Circle and includes members such as Buffet, Richard Branson, Donald Trump, Sara Blakely, (the youngest female billionaire), Bill Gates, and Steve Jobs. Even if you don't have the desire to become a billionaire, the success principles they use will lead you to success.

If you can get better at your job, you should be an active member of LinkedIn, because LinkedIn should be connecting you to the information, insights, and people to be more effective.

Reid Hoffman

Before 1954, nobody had run a mile in under four minutes. Many people, including doctors, believed it was impossible for a human being to run that fast. Roger Bannister ignored all of the naysayers and in 1954 broke the four-minute barrier. Since then, over 20,000 people, including high school students, have reached that seemingly unreachable goal.

Les Brown says that everything is possible. Everything you need is already inside you, waiting to be used. When you operate out of your imagination and not your memory, you will see possibilities everywhere and will be able to act on them.

Why it is important to me to show you that my awareness to the billionaires circle is twofold?

1. I didn't know that there are over 1,645 billionaires. Did you? Awareness is the first step to learning everything including yourself.

2. When you played the "I am" game (your character traits), you helped yourself get clear of who you are so you can authentically share with other in order for them to get to know you better. With millionaires and billionaires their characteristics and skills will help you to see, if you see greatness in others you can see it in yourself. What other possibilities could this create for you?

Here are a few billionaires

Giorgio Armani- Fashion Designer

Jeff Bezos- Amazon

Liliane Bittencourt- L'Oreal

Sara Blakley- Spanx (youngest female billionaire)

Michael Bloomberg- Bloomberg LP (stock market)

Donald Bren- Real Estate

Sergey Brin- Google

Warren Buffet- Berkshire Hathaway

Michael Dell- Dell computers

Larry Ellison-Oracle

Bill Gates- Microsoft

Reid Hoffman- LinkedIn

Steve Jobs- Apple

Phil Knight- Niki

Eric Lefkosky- Groupon

Forrest Mars- Candy

Dietrich Mateschitz- Red Bull

Howard Schultz- Starbucks

Donald Trump- Television, Real Estate

Christy Walton- Walmart

Ty Warner- Beanie Babies
Mark Zuckerberg- Facebook

Dee Beaudette 1st

President at Collective Changes, dedicated to supporting global women entrepreneurs through education and mentoring

Greater Seattle Area   Nonprofit Organization Management

Current	Collective Changes, Dee Beaudette Consulting, MacKenzie Romero Consulting
Previous	Peak Education, HIS Foundation, Webster International
Education	Independent Study - AFP Faculty Certification

Send a message   Endorse ▼

500+ connections

Gail M. Romero, CFRE 1st

CEO Collective Changes, NACC Past Board Chair, BM Gates Foundation - Advisor, Senior Counsel MacKenzie-Romero Consult

Greater Seattle Area   Executive Office

Current	Bill & Melinda Gates Foundation, Collective Changes - Global Mentoring, Rainmakers tv
Previous	MBA Women International, MBA Women International - formerly NAWMBA, Growing Philanthropy Summit
Education	AFP Faculty Training Academy

Send a message   Endorse ▼

500+ connections

Together we are more

Anytime I go somewhere I keep my ears open and my antennae up. I got an opportunity to go a very large women's conference in Long Beach, produced by Michelle Paterson and formerly produced by Maria Shriver in Long Beach.

Among the amazing speakers were Jack Canfield and Lisa Nichols. At one of the booths, I saw a banner that said Collective Changes and curiosity struck. "What was this odd thing about?" I thought. I saw the opportunity, reached out my hand, and said, "Hi, my name is Debra Faris, what's yours?" That's how I met Dee Beaudette.

I was excited as she told me about how Collective Changes became a Global non-profit corporation that empowers women in business through collaboration. "We use a unique on-line and mobile technology to match mentors and mentees. Then we guide them through tasks that build leadership and business skills," she said. "We launched in South Africa and then expanded to help women around the world build and sustain enterprises that create social, political and economic stability."

Dee met Gail in an on-line Master's program at Northpark University in Chicago. Since they both lived on the West Coast, they teamed up to do group projects. After eight years working in different cities, they decided to reconnect and follow their passion for empowering women. Collective Changes was born.

Collective Changes' primary target audience is the forgotten middle women in emerging countries who owning small to medium size enterprises. They complete a six-month program, then continue as associate and then full mentors building leadership skills in their communities.

Wajed "Roger" Salam

1st

Bus. Consultant ♦ Mastermind Forum Founder ♦ Joint Venture Expert ♦ Bestselling Author ♦ Speaker ♦ Social Entrepreneur

Tampa/St. Petersburg, Florida Area   Professional Training & Coaching

Current	The Winners Circle Mastermind Forum I Member: Ed Keels, The Winners Circle Mastermind Forum I Member: Dave Stech, The Winners Circle Mastermind Forum I Member: Glenn Dietzel
Previous	GEN International, Inc. (Tampa, FL, Germany, Australia), Foresight International (Tampa, FL, London, UK), Robbins Research International
Education	University of California, Los Angeles

Send a message   Endorse ▼   500+ connections

Imagine that you just took a trip around the world with eight of the smartest people in the world. Would you see things from a different perspective?

I met Roger Salam at a Tony Robbins event 30 years ago and knew without a shadow of doubt that he was a difference maker.

As years passed I decided to make a list of people I had met back then since I wondered where they were.

One by one found them. When Roger reappeared, I was not surprised that he had become an international speaker and author, worked directly with Tony Robbins, and did 3,700 talks. As founder of The Winner Circle runs the most unique mastermind event in the world at a 38,000 square-foot mansion.

Recently, I was part of an all the star lineup and got to speak at icon event with my long lost friend Roger "Wajed" Salem. Roger says that positioning is key when forming a mastermind group. You look at the end result you want to achieve as a whole to create your vision and mission. Individual goals may very but your core values and principles must align.

Roger says a core 100 people who are aligned can mastermind together and influence millions. My favorite quotes are, "Who you hang with, who you associate with, and who you listen to will determine your destiny" and "None of us is as smart as all of us."

Amazing Grace, a Pondering Thought

Amazing Grace by John Newton is an amazing song sung in hundreds of churches all over the world. Yet most people are not aware of the deep sorrow attached to it, the many lives that were lost, and the stories behind them. The even more astounding but extremely thought-provoking paradox is how we… you… me… each one of us… can change or be difference makers.

In the mid eighteenth century, John Newton, age 22, was a slave trader exporting human lives from West Africa to South Carolina on his own slave ship. One night he had a dramatic faith experience during a storm at sea. Following that storm he gave his life to God and began to read spiritual books and pray. He continued to run his slave ships, making three more voyages. Two days before his fourth voyage was to set sail, a mysterious illness temporarily paralyzed him. He never made the fourth journey.

That experience changed his life, which changed his thinking. He became a pastor who opposed the slave trade. In 1788 he met William Wilberforce, an influential Member of Parliament, and began to mentor him on the slave trade. The two men collaborated in a campaign to outlaw the slave trade. In 1807 the once sinner Newton along with Wilberforce and their colleagues prevailed when Parliament voted to outlaw the slave trade in Britain. He almost single handedly abolished slavery. The sinner became one of the most influential humanitarians of his time and the ripple effect of his actions changed the world.

Most of us fail to question how it happens that people can create such devastating life events as slavery and how we can prevent such moral failings in the future. John Newton was born into the slave trade. At the age of 11 in 1743, he went to sea with his father to Jamaica as a slave master. He became a midshipman, was demoted for trying to desert, and then returned to West Africa on another slave ship.

Many people go through tragedies and hardships that other people who haven't walked in their shoes cannot understand. These others are filled with judgment and criticism because they take their everyday freedom for granted and do not realize what it took for the person they criticize to get where they are.

We all have been involved in judgment and criticism and even condemnation toward another person because we believe they should or should not have done something

Dr. Wayne Dyer shared in his program *Wishes Fulfilled* that as soon as he let go his self-defeating inflections, he created miracles in his life. We are all just doing what we know how to do.(paraphrased) "We must let go of any thoughts of judgment, criticism or condemnation. We are all God's children," he says.

Let's recap

*The **words of character** that resonate with me are:*
<u>Vision</u>, <u>Wisdom</u>, <u>Honorable</u>

*What **character words** could you add about yourself?*

1._____ 2._____ 3._____

*The **mentor/coach** I think of is <u>Mahatma Gandhi.</u>*

What mentor/coach do you think of? _____

Recommended Book:
Think and Grow Rich by Napoleon Hill

Commencements – John F. Kennedy
http://www.youtube.com /watch?v=GnCps4GHGmY

After you watched the YouTube video, what inspired you?

Your thoughts: _____

Thank You, to all who touch you

Remember, little Thank Yous could be the only positive thing that happened in that person's life that day. When we are grateful for the little things, our life is abundant and when we believe we live in a friendly peaceful world, we feel peace. I want to thank you for being our leaders and our creators that will make our world a better place tomorrow. I would also like to give thanks to the people and industries in my life. To name a few here:

My Children and Family: Phil (in loving memory) Dan, Gina, Phil's Princess Denise, Phil's Girls (Scarlet & Sophie) Gina's husband Dom and their son August :) RIP: Aunt Marge Elison, my Dad and my Mom.

My Friends: Lee Pound, Bob Bare, Jack C. Crawford, Bob Donnell, Cindy Vaughn, Lori Hart, Bruce Carse, Michael J. Herman. June Davidson, my Life Coach Joseph

All my friends on LinkedIn,

All the people that serve us in their chosen careers

Airlines/Aviation, Art/Creators, Athletics/Sports, Auto, Biotechnology, Business Owners/Consultants, Construction, Consumer Electronics, Energies, Entertainment,/T.V. Film/Music, Environmental Services, Farming Business Owner, Fashion/Apparel/Beauty, Finance World, Angel investors, Founders, Green Technology, Higher Education, History, Import/Export, Insurance, International trade, Law Enforcement, Law, Food/Beverage, Libraries, Consumer Goods, Management, C-Level, Manufacturing, Marketing, Military, Non Profit, Non-Profit, Patient Creators, Peace Makers, Plastics, Real Estate, Service Industries, Retail, Staffing, Technology, Telecommunications, Travel

Lee Pound, you are the whole enchilada; a brilliant writer, grammatical king, patients of a saint, work ethics of a Thomas Edison support like a Dallas Cowboys cheerleader, instincts like a tiger and heart like Leo Buscaglia. I don't know what I did to be so lucky to have a prince like you, but grateful and humble. You are my man Genie in a bottle. :)

Bob Bare, thank you for believing in my vision to make a difference to college students.

Jack C. Crawford, life is full of surprises and you were one of mine. Anyone can make a difference when it means something to them, you made me feel like I can make a difference. Thank you for your generosity in getting me back up and running when my computer crashed. You stopped your life for me when you had so much on your own plate to be sure this book would become a reality.

Joseph, when others don't see someone's broken heart you saw mine and when I could see the light you turned it on. I am forever grateful for your life coaching. I know that my son would have picked you to help me put back the pieces.

Gary Kissel, words can't express how you were the night in shining armor to give us another pair of eyes from that 30,000-foot view. You helped us shine our treasure to give the gift of having someone who knows LinkedIn like you help us gussy it up like a celebrity getting dressed for the academy awards.

My Professors, Mentors, Trainers, Coaches, and Authors
Jay Abraham, Carol Adrienne, Mitch Albom, David Bach, Byrd
Baggett, Lucille Ball, Sara Blakley, Kenneth Blanchard Ph.D,
Sheldon Bowles, Richard Branson, Kingdon L. Brown, Rene Buce,
Warren Buffet, Bob Burg, George Burns, Jack Canfield, Dale
Carnegie, Jerome Carter, Carlos Castaneda, Vivian Clecak, Deepak
Chopra, Steven Covey, Robert Crisp, William D. Danko Ph.D., Eli
Davidson, Bob Davies, Dr. John Demartini, Walt Disney, Bob
Donnell, Todd Duncan, Craig Duswalt, Wayne Dyer, Thomas
Edison, Jeff Eggers, Albert Einstein, Ralph Waldo Emerson, David
Fagan, Mike Ferry™, Henry Ford, Patricia Fripp, Mahatma Gandhi,
Bill Gates, Shakti Gawain, Michael E. Gerber, JD Gershbein, Jeffrey
Gitomer, Mark Victor Hansen, Stephanie Havelka, George Hess,
Napoleon Hill, Don Hobbs, Jeff Hoffman, Tom Hopkins, Robert
Irvine, Steve Jobs Foundation, Spencer Johnson, C G Jung, Kahn
Education, Gary Keller, Hellen Keller, Laurel King, John LaBonte,
Loral Langemeier, Abraham Lincoln, Niccolo Machiavelli, James
Malinchak, Christopher Maurer, Maxwell Maltz, Og Mandino, John
C. Maxwell, Kevin W. McCarthy, Dr. Joseph Murphy, John Newton,
Donald Norfolk, Jim Palmer, Norman Vincent Peale, Plato, Price
Pritchett, Bob Proctor, Karen Rager, David Richo Ph.D, Tony
Robbins, Jim Rohn, Sanaya Roman, Felipe Ruiz, Robert H. Schuller,
Hyrum W. Smith, Socrates, Jonathan Sprinkles, Thomas J.Stanley
Ph.D, Brian Tracy, Donald Trump, Peter Vessenes, Dr. Denis
Waitley, Dottie Walters, Rick Warren, Stuart Wilde, Bruce
Wilkinson, Oprah Winfrey, Zig Ziglar,

Other Contributors
Jessica Gillette, Shannon Castello, Cherie Kaylor,
Victoria Reynolds, Bob Maxwell, Kobe Dumas, Avi Shaid, Robert
Flegal, Steve McNally, Cindy Pickens
For more information:
www.linkedinforcollegestudents.com   www.debrafaris.com
Join me on LinkedIn, Facebook, and Twitter

U.C.B.
LIBRARY

Lightning Source UK Ltd.
Milton Keynes UK
UKOW06f0352101215

264408UK00016B/343/P

9 781619 200265